Trajectory

*My Twelve-Year Battle with the
Canadian Armed Forces*

R. Douglas McBride

FriesenPress

Suite 300 - 990 Fort St
Victoria, BC, Canada, V8V 3K2
www.friesenpress.com

Author photo by impactdigitalphotography.com

Trajectoryproject.net

ISBN
978-1-4602-6923-7 (Hardcover)
978-1-4602-6924-4 (Paperback)
978-1-4602-6925-1 (eBook)

1. BIOGRAPHY & AUTOBIOGRAPHY, Lawyers & Judges
2. BIOGRAPHY & AUTOBIOGRAPHY, Military
3. LAW, Military

Distributed to the trade by The Ingram Book Company

for Kerry who has stood by me the entire time

Contents

Foreword

Colonel Michel W. Drapeau (Retired)

As a former commissioned armed forces officer, a lawyer specializing in Canadian military law, and author and lecturer in Canadian
military law, I am neither dismayed nor surprised by the disturbing
account chronicled in this book by the father of a man, Andrew
McBride, who enrolled in the Canadian Forces in 1995, first as
a Cadet at the Royal Military College (RMC) in Kingston where
he graduated with a Baccalaureate in Arts (Military and Strategic
Studies) and who went on to serve with the Royal Regiment of the
Canadian Artillery. However, his career was derailed and eventually demolished as a result of a most minor conflict with one of
his immediate superiors in a training exercise which took place
in Camp Gagetown, New Brunswick. This minor dispute mush
room led not only to a course failure but his eventual compulsory
release from the army. Until his release from the military in 2007,
Second- Lieutenant Andrew McBride, ably assisted by his lawyer-
father, mounted several grievances and submissions within both
the CF Grievance Process and the CF Career Administrative
Review process, but to no avail. His search for justice and fairness
led him also to apply to the Federal Courts for judicial review, but
again all was for naught. Marginalized, railroaded, stonewalled,
deceived, bullied and lied to by his military superiors, this led to

a serious degradation of his health. In the end, Andrew was medically released.

Having served in the Canadian military for thirty-four years and now in the active practice of law specializing in military law, I read this well-written, compelling manuscript with much interest but with an increasing level of disappointment, exasperation and angst. The narration of the deep-seated flaws of the military justice system, the obvious and dramatic lack of natural justice and procedural fairness in both the grievance and the exhaustive but deeply biased CF career review procedure, the lack of candour and transparency, and the sheer and shameless repudiation of the much vaunted foundational values of honesty, courage, honour and integrity which are the provinces of the military profession are not unique to this story. I am regularly faced with similar accounts in my military law practice.

This book is not an attack upon the armed forces, nor is it upon any of the senior military commanders who collectively played a part in the destruction of a young man's career who was full of promise; a graduate of our much acclaimed Royal Military College who possessed an abundance of energy, loyalty, dedication, professional knowledge and *savoir-faire* which the armed forces officer corps desperately needs to meet Canada's multiple defence tasks. This book is also not about military incompetence. Unfortunately, it is much worse. At its core, it exposes the fundamental lack of officer-like qualities of some specific named individual officers and flawed ethics or a lethargic attitude on the part of many more.

Simply put, this book is a contemporary story detailing how a minority of Canadian Forces senior and junior officers who appear to be lacking some of the essential virtues required to hold commissioned rank so as to discharge the onerous duty to command and lead subordinates were, nonetheless, vouchsafed by being given an unfettered amount of power, allowing them to manipulate the military career administration system to eventually forcibly retire or otherwise curtail the career progression of a young aspiring junior whose only fault may have been his inability to conceal his lights

beneath the bushels of conformity which led to a cascade of opposi-
tional procedures.

This McBride story painfully illustrates, in abundant detail, the
authoritarian tendencies and the ritualistic dominance-submission
relationship of the military towards its subordinates. More à propos,
it lays out the *modus operandi* of the Canadian military justice system
including the grievance system which has shown, in statuesque pro-
portions, its incapacity to provide justice and to redress wrongs.

More than anything, the book exposes a military justice system
which is currently an insult to the birth rights of ordinary Canadians
and their legitimate expectations that their sons and daughters who
serve in the Canadian Forces will be treated with respect by a fair,
open and impartial justice system. Instead, it lays bare the abject
failure of the Canadian Forces Grievance Process by revealing the
existence of layers of senior military leaders who have exhibited
either wilful blindness or an unforgettable detachment from their
commissioned duty to look after subordinates in a fair manner.
Provided with several opportunities to conduct a *de novo* review,
the McBrides' *cris de Coeur* were simply drowned by waves of yawns
by the military. The officer corps simply watched, in slow motion,
the annihilation of the budding career of Andrew McBride whose
early military career showed a great deal of promise.

In my considered opinion, this story encapsulates what's wrong
with the military administrative law system which is an integral
part of the military justice system, namely, significant and regular
breaches by commissioned officers of the much hailed code of
values and code of ethics; a sluggish senior leadership abstracted to
such breaches; and the bulldozing of subordinates who must
endure such excesses without either a right to representation or an
authentic and reliable grievance procedure. Much worse, however,
it presents a chilling portrait of how the "system", which transcends
all levels of commands, rigged the truth in McBride's case in order
to arrive at a determined slapdash outcome. After all, in an authori-
tative regime such as the Canadian Forces, it is a lot easier to protect

the 'brand' than to dare expose flaws in the system or challenge the status quo.

If I were a rich man, I would purchase a copy of this book and provide it as required reading to every commissioned officer above the rank of major. If I were a powerful man, however, I would first order a book for the Minister, the Chief of the Defence Staff, and for the senior commanders as well as the Chief of Military Personnel and ask each of them to prepare an essay on this failure of generalship and officership. I would then order the re-engineering of CF Grievance System so as to have both the Minister of National Defence and the Chief of the Defence Staff be, once again, part of the grievance chain to ensure that they gain a panoramic perspective, as the circumstances demand, to any such catastrophic failures of the military justice system and the military career administration process.

If nothing else, this grim story is but one more example of the urgent need to bring fresh oxygen to the military justice system because, as noted by the father of another doomed young serviceman in an Opinion Piece published in the Ottawa Citizen on March 7, 2015:

> *Absolute power apparently does corrupt and that is at the root of the problem. Soldiers are subjected to a closed military justice system which in our experience protects the chain of command and political masters and is impermeable to civilian oversight. As a result the military is not answerable or open in their actions. It is unclear if they are simply rogue or falling on their sword when their conduct has become arrogant and egregious… We are an open democracy not some dictatorship where that type of high handed conduct might be tolerated.*

Shaun Fynes, Victoria, British Columbia

Not only does this case beg for justice, but the entire military administrative law landscape as conceived needs to be reviewed by a board or commission of inquiry so that important changes to the workings of the system can be brought to bear. To the skeptical I say this: If the military can, with characteristic obstinacy and resoluteness, inflict so much pain and destruction on a young commissioned officer in peacetime, imagine what it can do when the forces are deployed abroad on operations where a combination of secrecy, security and patriotism would provide the military with an ungoverned use of its considerable legal and disciplinary powers to impose its will on defenceless junior ranks. Scary.

A must read for readers not previously versed in the military bureaucracy who wish to gain an insight into the military mind and its irrational authoritarianism, dogmatism as well as autocratic behaviour. The author is to be congratulated for having had the skills and the fortitude to present a powerful story which might serve to alert a new generation of Canadians who might be tempted to make a career in the armed forces. More importantly, however, the book will most certainly serve to inform the political class and tomorrow's military leaders of the need for significant reforms to the broken military justice system including the CF grievance system which, in its present configuration, allows such a disgraceful treatment of an aspiring officer.

—

Colonel Michel W. Drapeau, OMM, CD, LL.L., LL.B. served for thirty-four years in the Canadian Forces, retiring in 1993 from the dual appointment of Director, Executive Secretary, National Defence Headquarters and Secretary, Armed Forces Council. In retirement, he earned a degree in Civil Law and one in Common Law. He articled at the Federal Court of Appeal. He established his law practice in Ottawa specializing in administrative law. He was named Adjunct Professor. Faculty of Law, University of Ottawa in 2009. He is the author or co-author of several legal texts including *Military Justice in Action*, Thompson-Carswell, 2015. He currently serves on the Board of Administration, St-Paul University, Ottawa, Ontario.

A brief introduction

There is, by nature of its content, a great deal of terminology in this book, and so rather than have the reader struggle needlessly, I thought I might take a moment here to touch on some of it in advance.

What's in a name?

In 1968 the Royal Canadian Navy and Royal Canadian Air Force dropped their royal monikers and became the Canadian Navy and Air Force. The unified navy, air force and army were then known as Canadian Armed Forces.

In the nineties, the Canadian Armed Forces saw dramatic funding cuts under Prime Minister Chretien. Canada's role was framed primarily as a peacekeeping force (requiring, not coincidentally, far less in the way of military spending) and the Canadian Armed Forces were rebranded as the Canadian Forces.

Unfortunately, though the world spins like inexorable clockwork on its axis, the state of play on the ground is not so predictable, and in both Europe and the Middle East, Canada's role would not be neatly confined to peacekeeping.

In 2011, under Prime Minister Harper and Defence Minister Peter MacKay, the Royal designation was restored to the navy and air force (to the ire of some, especially in Québec). And in 2013, the Canadian Forces was once again rebranded as the Canadian *Armed* Forces.

In *Trajectory*, I will be using the name Canadian Forces (CF), for that is what they were called during Andrew's (and my) involvement with them.

Ranks

Andrew's time in CF was spent in the army. For those readers who are unfamiliar with the progression of ranks in the Canadian Army, I provide them here along with their accepted abbreviations. There are a great number of players in this story, and most of them were army officers.

Officer Cadet	Ocdt
Second Lieutenant	2Lt
Lieutenant	Lt
Captain	Capt
Major	Maj
Lieutenant-Colonel	LCol
Colonel	Col
Brigadier-General	BGen
Major-General	MGen
Lieutenant-General	LGen
General	Gen

Acronyms

Finally, it should come as no surprise, even to readers relatively unfamiliar with the armed forces, that life in the military is replete with acronyms. I will endeavour to keep these under control within the manuscript and offer parenthetical explanations where appropriate. As a quick reference, however, here is a list of some of the acronyms that have made their way into the text.

AR	Administrative Review
ASU	Area Support Unit
BC	Battery Commander
CDS	Chief of the Defence Staff
CF	Canadian Forces
CFB	Canadian Forces Base
CFGB	Canadian Forces Grievance Board
Cmdt	Commandant
CO	Commanding Officer
COS	Chief of Staff
Comd	Commander
CP	Command Post
CPO	Command Post Officer (Artillery)
CTC	Combat Training Centre
DCFGA	Director Canadian Forces Grievance Authority
DGMC	Director General Military Careers
DMCARM	Director Military Careers Administration and Resource Management
D Med Pol	Director Medical Policy
DOJ	Department of Justice
FA	Final Authority

FOO	Forward Observation Officer
GPO	Gun Positioning Officer
IA	Initial Authority
JAG	Judge Advocate General
MEL	Medical Employment Limitation
MO	Medical Officer
NDHQ	National Defence Headquarters
PRB	Progress Review Board
Regt	Regiment
ROTP	Regular Officer Training Program
SITREP	Situation Report
U of S	Universality of Service

tra·jec·to·ry *noun:*

the path followed by an object in flight given the forces
acting upon it

Prologue

I landed at Fredericton International on the afternoon of August 2,
2001. It was a Thursday. I was tired, having taken a direct flight from
Vancouver International in order to attend my son's graduation the
following week. A second lieutenant in the Second Regiment, Royal
Canadian Horse Artillery out of Petawawa, Andrew had spent the
summer at the Combat Training Centre in Gagetown in order to
complete his Basic Artillery Officer training thus becoming a fully
qualified Gun Positioning Officer.

The plan was to stay in the barracks and attend his graduation
and then split the driving with Andrew when he packed up and
headed back to Petawawa.

I was excited for him and, as always, immensely proud of his
accomplishments. He had wanted nothing so much as a career in
the Canadian Forces since before he was old enough to join the
cadets, and his drive and determination had certainly served him
well. At twenty-four my son had already been pursuing this dream
for half his life. This was but another step along the path.

Andrew met me at arrivals, and I could tell as soon as I saw him that something was on his mind. I hadn't seen him since Christmas, and he looked, to me, a little drawn. I knew that the CTC courses were often gruelling and had come to expect the greeting of a young man who'd been put through his paces. But there was something else going on.

We loaded my bags into Andrew's car and headed to Gagetown for a private end-of-course barbecue. Leaving the airport, most of the traffic turned west towards Fredericton; we turned east. It's not a long drive to the base, and so I wasn't surprised when Andrew pulled off onto the shoulder just before the iron bridge over the Oromocto river.

"So," I said.

Andrew gripped the wheel as if unsure where to start. The windows were open, and the breeze off the asphalt was warm. An SUV drove by and crossed the bridge, the deep bass of its sound system beating like a frantic heart, and in the ensuing silence, a cicada hidden high in one of the scrubby poplars off the side of the road began to keen.

Part 1:
Taking Aim

One

In June of 1982, my son Andrew turned five. It was during the Falkland Islands conflict, and I remember him sitting with me and my friend, Charlie Whisker, as we watched coverage play out on the CBC. Though Andrew wouldn't have been up for *The National* or *The Journal,* he would have been there in the living room for the six o'clock news, especially if Charlie was over. Charlie, a high school teacher who taught History 12, was great with kids. He was also Captain Whisker with the local Army Cadet Corps and had a lot to say about what was unfolding in the South Atlantic.

—

I had moved to Nanaimo from the BC interior ten years earlier to practise law closer to the woman I loved. Kerry Gorbatuk was from Powell River, and she and I had met in 1970 when I was in Powell River visiting my folks—the Gorbatuks, as it turned out, lived a block away from the McBrides. In the summer of 1970, I was between my second and third year as a law student and was an auxiliary RCMP officer in Nelson.

Back in 1968, I had applied to both the RCMP and law school and had been accepted in both. Determined not to forego the former for the latter, it was suggested I become an auxiliary officer in the meantime. As it turned out, an accident in 1969 badly injured my knee, and after the surgeries it was clear that my chance of actually pursuing a career in the RCMP was over.

In 1971, I articled with Angene Miller in Nelson and was called to the bar on May 15, 1972. Kerry and I were engaged the same day. By then I had put over 18,000 miles on my poor old VW Beetle and was tired of trekking back and forth, so when an opportunity to do family law in Nanaimo at Strongitharm Miller Currie & Ramsay came up, I jumped at it. Kerry and I were married in 1973 and, in 1974, purchased a modest home on Garner Crescent that backed onto a then-undeveloped ridge and offered us a good view of Mount Benson.

Kerry first met Charlie Whisker in 1974 when she interned with him at Woodlands Secondary to complete her teacher's certificate. The three of us hit it off right away. She would start teaching math and social studies at Woodlands that fall, but three years later decided to become a stay-at-home mom when Andrew was born.

I left Strongitharm Miller Currie & Ramsay and went out on my own in March of 1977—this was three months before Andrew was born. I was a young guy with a lot of progressive ideas about how things should be done, and I had made enough of a name for myself that I thought I could make a go of it. Peter Ramsay felt I had made the right move, and in a few years we had built McBride Ramsay Thompson Lampman.

Kerry and I had a second son, Stephan, in September of 1979.

—

By the time Andrew was going into first grade, Kerry and I suspected that computers would play a big role in the lives of his generation, so when he was six, he was given his first computer. It was a Commodore 64, and he took to it right away—his favourite game, when it came out four years later, would be *Airborne Ranger.*

Like most kids, Andrew and his brother had rich, active imaginations, and there were persistent military motifs running through their make-believe worlds and play. GI Joe and little plastic army men were certainly always to be found among the toys at the McBride household. The boys had a shed in the back yard, and it was always their fort. We had a summer property on Cortes Island in Desolation Sound, and right across the Lewis Channel from us—about four kilometres away on a small islet at the entrance to West Redonda Island's Refuge Cove—was the local Sea Cadets base. The boys would watch the cadet ships come and go with great interest and soon established their own "Navy Base" on the eastern shore of Cortes.

There is a photo from Cortes (this would have been before the navy base) of a five-year-old Andrew in swim trunks and running shoes, standing atop a raft that was nothing more than a couple of pieces of waterlogged timber placed unevenly astride two logs resting in less than a foot of water. Andrew's right hand is set high on a surf-stripped branch as thick as his arm and almost twice as tall as he is. His left hand is on his hip, and he looks as though he is getting ready to pole out across the channel. Behind him to the east, the hills of West Redonda crowd the horizon.

For Andrew, life was an adventure, and he was a kid who was all too happy to meet it head on. Perhaps it was that sense of adventure that often drew his imagination to military themes. If there was one event that truly hooked him, however, it was an army cadet demonstration I took him and his brother to in March of 1989. I'm sure it was Charlie who tipped us off to the event—Captain Whisker was, by then, commanding the Nanaimo 2422 Cadet Corps out of the Nanaimo Military Camp on 5th Street.

For cadets to participate in para training in the summer months, they had to be thoroughly evaluated, as you'd expect, to ensure that they'd be up to it. The hopeful candidates, having been selected, would all come together during spring break and go through a rigorous week of activities. At the end of the week, they put on a demonstration for the public, and it was this demonstration that sealed the deal for Andrew. At eleven years old, he saw something that day that spoke to him. Perhaps the sight of those young cadets connected some dots in his imagination and suggested a bridge to something more than simply play and make-believe.

In June, Andrew turned twelve. That September, Kerry returned to teaching, and Andrew joined the Canadian Scottish Regiment 2422 Army Cadets. I still remember picking Andrew up after his first night at cadets. He and the other new cadets had been issued their kit (different uniforms) and it was a lot for a twelve-year-old kid to carry. I remember him dropping something as he walked to the car, stooping to pick it up, and dropping something else in the process. Every year thereafter, I would see a new crop of twelve-year-olds struggling with their kit after the first night. It always made me smile.

Watching cadets mature from kids into young adults over the years was always something to behold. It's probably not widely appreciated, but the cadet programs really are wonderful. These are structured programs for kids between the ages of twelve and eighteen that keep them physically fit, challenged and engaged. They encourage kids to focus and strive and become civic minded, and they teach a wide range of skills they can use for the rest of their life. While it's true that a lot of kids go on from cadets to enrol in the Canadian Forces, there really is no expectation that they do so.

Andrew loved cadets. He never served under Captain Whisker though, for in September of 1989, Charlie had just stepped down as the cadet CO though he remained active in the unit. By the time Stephan joined in 1991, the 2422 was under the command of Lieutenant R. C. Welbourn. After Charlie retired from teaching in 1993, Captain Whisker was made a Major responsible for all the army cadets on the island. He was always proud, I think, that our kids had joined *his unit*, and he always kept his eye on their progress.

Cadets was so good for Andrew and Stephan that Kerry and I decided to keep them in public school rather than sending them to Brentwood, a boarding school north of Victoria on the Saanich Inlet, just so they could continue to participate.

We decided that, as conscientious involved parents, one of whom had a teacher's certificate, we'd be able to make sure they got the most out of their time at Nanaimo District Secondary School. For us, part of that meant always making sure that they had state-of-the-art computers. In 1989, for instance, I got Hennessey Systems to build us a top-of-the-line machine with the brand new 486 chip. I remember Lionel who came to install it turning to wide-eyed Andrew (12) and Stephan (10) and solemnly trying to impress upon them that this was a powerful computer and not a toy—the boys nodding and grinning. At the time, that machine cost us just over ten thousand dollars; it had a staggering 8 MB of RAM.

When it came to their involvement in cadets, Andrew and Stephan always got a lot of recognition from their Uncle Paul. Kerry's younger brother had, in his day, been the top army cadet in BC and loved to talk about attending the Banff Army Cadet Camp for a summer of climbing on the Columbia Icefield.

Andrew was a fiercely dedicated cadet and a kid who, in all aspects of his life, liked to challenge himself and set personal goals. In early 1992, he read about *Canada 125* in the newspaper. It was a national program, celebrating the Canada's Quasquicentennial, intended to bring youth from across Canada together to explore either the centres of national power (Ottawa, Toronto, Québec City, and Montréal) or the space program (Québec).

Andrew asked for the forms at school but was told they had been thrown out since there weren't any students who would qualify for the program. I'm not entirely sure of how *that* conversation went, but the forms were retrieved from the garbage and given to Andrew. I remember being quite proud of Andrew for taking the initiative like that when the school had dropped the ball and sold its students short. Andrew was fourteen when he did this.

Applicants had to answer a questionnaire and write an essay. Andrew applied to both arms of the program and was accepted in both. The only fly in the ointment was that we would be attending an army cadet camp that summer as part of the Cadet Leader

Instructor course and would need to obtain permission to leave early. The cadets were only too happy to accommodate Andrew. And so that summer, we drove to Vernon to pick him up and got him on a plane in Kelowna so he could connect with a flight out of Vancouver that would take him east.

He came back from *Canada 125* with some terrific memories and an astronaut flight suit, if you can believe it. There is a picture somewhere of Andrew wearing his flight suit flanked by a couple of younger cousins who were clearly impressed.

Andrew and Stephan attended summer cadet camps every year. Like his uncle Paul had years before, Andrew attended the Banff Army Cadet "Leadership and Challenge" camp and spent a summer on the Columbia Icefield, one of only two hundred cadets chosen from twenty-two thousand cadets across Canada. Another year, he was a cadet leader in a ten-day wilderness expedition to climb the Golden Hinde—Vancouver Island's highest peak at 2,195 metres— and was one of only two cadets to reach the summit. He ended his time with the cadets as a Warrant Officer. Cadets was his life, and he thrived on the challenges.

In Andrew's last year of high school, Kerry brought the Euclid math contest to his attention. She was a math teacher, remember, and well aware of what Andrew was capable of. True, this was a challenging contest run out of the University of Waterloo, but she knew her son well enough to know that the challenge would motivate him. Andrew enquired at school and was told that, yes, there was such a contest but he would not do well as it was quite advanced. Nothing could have motivated him more than that. He entered and progressed through the levels of the contest and was awarded a certificate of distinction.

Andrew was always a strong-willed student and resisted wasting his time on things he felt he didn't need to know. He actually finished grade twelve a term early by challenging a number of courses— opting to test for a credit without taking the course. During his extra down time, he took a couple of first year courses (math and physics) at Malaspina College. I also hired Charlie Whisker (now retired) to come in and give Andrew an intensive history course highlighting Canadian military history. He was not a kid to rest on his laurels.

Andrew had applied to join CF in the fall of his grade twelve year. He was seventeen years old and applied for the Regular Officer Training Program (ROTP) with Officer Candidate Training Program (OCTP) as a backup with enrolment as a private in the Regular forces as a backup to *that*.

Applicants had to complete a number of assessments, including a math test that had to be completed in an hour. Andrew handed it back in ten minutes and was challenged on whether he could have completed it. He had, and when it was marked, obtained 100%. The recruiter remarked that he had never seen a perfect mark obtained on the test.

I remember Kerry and I had to check in with CF recruiting at the time of Andrew's swearing in. We were greeted at the counter by the man who had recently taken over the Victoria CF Recruitment Office, a young Navy Lieutenant by the name of Robert Ferguson, and when Andrew explained who we were, Lt (N) Ferguson said, "So *you're* McBride."

Uh oh, I thought, *what does* that *mean?*

The man smiled. "We've never had *anyone* apply to enrol in so many ways simultaneously."

Andrew had, in fact, been accepted into the ROTP and was sworn in as an officer cadet at CFB Esquimalt on June 8, 1995. He was three days shy of his eighteenth birthday when he recited the Oath of Allegiance.

> "I, Robert Andrew McBride, do swear that I will be faithful and bear true allegiance to Her Majesty Queen Elizabeth the Second, Queen of Canada, Her Heirs and Successors. So help me God."

Andrew had requested infantry, but was assigned to artillery due to his excellent math abilities.

At the time, all ROTP officer cadets began their training in British Columbia's lush Fraser Valley at CFB Chilliwack before attending Royal Military College in Kingston in the fall. Formerly Camp Chilliwack, CFB Chilliwack stood on a parcel of land in the community of Vedder Crossing just south of the city of Chilliwack and north of the Vedder river—it was renamed in 1968 to reflect the newly-unified Canadian Armed Forces (and closed in 1997 due to budget cuts).

The Canadian Forces Officer Training School at CFB Chilliwack ran the Basic Officer Training Course for all three branches of CF. BOTC includes all the physical rigours of basic training with additional emphasis placed on leadership skills. For Andrew and fellow officer cadets, days started at 5:00 a.m. and ended at 11:00 p.m. and consisted of intense physical training, field exercises, obstacle courses and fitness evaluations. The course ran Monday to Friday through July and August with officer cadets being confined to barracks for the first weekend and confined to base for the second and third weekends.

The motto of CFB Chilliwack was *Achievement*, and that seems apt considering the rigours officer cadets were subjected to. Included among the fitness evaluations of the Basic Officer Training Course is the Battlefield Fitness Test. In it candidates must complete a 13km hike in full gear weighing 24.5 kg in less than 2 hours and 26 minutes. In 1995, Andrew was one of the few cadets to successfully do so—the course had been incorrectly measured out that year and was in fact 16km. Officer Cadet McBride came through Basic Officer Training rightfully known as one of the hardcore cadets.

Kerry and I attended the graduation parade at CFB Chilliwack in August. Kerry then flew home from Abbotsford, but I stayed behind to drive Andrew and a mate back to Nanaimo so they could unpack and repack for RMC. Then we picked up another comrade in Victoria, and I got them all to Vancouver and onto a plane bound for Kingston.

Two

In the fall of 1995, Royal Military College (RMC) in Kingston was the only military school in Canada; earlier that year both the Collège Militaire Royal de Saint-Jean (CMR) and Vancouver Island's Royal Roads Military College (RRMC) had been closed due budget cuts. This meant that the ROTP applicants, that year, came to Kingston from all across Canada. Some, like Andrew, came from a cadet background, and that served them well, but many didn't, and for them it was likely more of a culture shock.

The Royal Military College of Canada, as it is now known, is located on a small peninsula at the mouth of Kingston Harbour between Fort Henry and downtown Kingston, Ontario. Established in 1876, it is empowered to confer degrees in arts, science and engineering.

It's mission statement:

> The Royal Military College of Canada, Canada's Military University, prepares officer-cadets for a career in the profession of arms and continues the development of other Canadian Forces members and civilians with interest in defence issues. RMC provides programs and courses of higher education and professional development to meet the needs of the Canadian Forces and the Department of National Defence.

RMC is charged with training officer cadets in what the CF considers to be the four pillars of military success, namely academics, officership, athletics, and bilingualism. The RMC motto: *Truth, Duty, Valour.*

Andrew kept himself very busy during his time at RMC. Apart from pursuing a four-year degree in Military and Strategic Studies, he participated in Aikido and took private scuba and parachuting classes. He was the commander of the RMC Precision Drill Team, a team which he himself initiated and led on its first visit to the US Military Academy at West Point. He also initiated and twice led an RMC team in the North American Model UN simulations, coming in second the first year and third the next.

Shortly after he arrived, Andrew used a Canada Student Loan to purchase a state-of-the-art computer so cutting edge that the IT department asked to have it for a few days upon its arrival. It was a custom build ordered through Dell, and no one in IT had ever gotten their hands on a computer that powerful. Andrew and his brother were both quite computer savvy by that point. In fact, Andrew had been building and upgrading computers for himself and his friends for a number of years.

—

In his first year at Royal Military College, on top of the first-year courses required for his degree and his many extra-curricular activities, Andrew successfully completed his basic officer training which amounted to the introductory-level Basic Artillery Officer training or BAO—Andrew would need to complete three more levels of artillery officer training to become a fully-qualified artillery officer. All of the remaining artillery officer training would take place at the Combat Training Centre at 5th Canadian Division Support Base Gagetown near Fredericton. This training was slated to take place over the second and third summers of his time at RMC and would wrap up the summer immediately after he graduated.

His first summer, however, he spent at Saint-Jean-sur-Richelieu just outside of Montréal, attending the Canadian Forces Language School still housed there. As the Collège Militaire Royal had been closed, he and the other students were housed in the Megastructure at Place Bonaventure and transported daily to the facilities.

—

During his second year at RMC, Andrew kept himself very busy with his studies and many extracurricular activities. In spring of 1997, Andrew read that CF had purchased the JANUS combat simulation system and that, furthermore, it was located at the Combat Training Centre at Gagetown. You want to bet that *that* piece of information registered on Andrew's radar.

JANUS was not new. It had originally been developed back in the seventies to model nuclear effects on combat forces and had been, in the intervening years, expanded and improved. By 1997 it was the most widely adopted military war game system available. Named after the Roman god of transitions—a two-faced deity able to look forwards and backwards simultaneously—JANUS was what is known as a deterministic simulation. It allowed for virtual simulations of large multi-sided combat engagements, where the results were entirely dependent on the decision-making of the participants. It generated realistic battlefield conditions and offered after-action review of results. The need to react to decisions made by human-controlled opposing forces in a realistic simulation meant that JANUS exercises were incredibly valuable. This was a far cry from *Airborne Ranger*, and for Andrew, the chance to test his mettle on JANUS was almost too good to be true.

When he had finished his second year at RMC, it was time to head east to take the first of three courses at Gagetown. Basic Artillery Officer II would pick up where his first year training left off.

New Brunswick's CFB Gagetown (more accurately known as 5th Canadian Division Support Base Gagetown) started as a Cold War military camp. When it was first created in the late fifties, a number of small communities needed to be expropriated to due to the scale of the training area planned. At the time, Gagetown was the largest military base and training facility in Canada; now it is second after CFB Suffield in Alberta. CFB Gagetown currently covers approximately 1,100 square kilometres of forest, swamps, marshlands, and open fields and contains live-fire ranges for infantry, armoured and artillery units. Its base proper is located in the northwest corner near the town of Oromocto, New Brunswick, approximately eighteen kilometres southeast of Fredericton and employs somewhere in the neighbourhood of 6,000 military and civilian personnel. Home to five operation units, it is also headquarters the CTC or Combat Training Centre, which conducts courses for over 15,000 Regular Force and Reserve Force students every year.

Andrew arrived at CFB Gagetown in May of 1997 to begin his BAO II. The courses were full time, running Monday to Friday, but were generally not as rigorous as the eighteen-hour days of basic officer training at CFB Chilliwack. Class time was spent in the massive training complex on the base itself, and it was during a morning coffee break that Andrew was able to find the as-of-yet-unmarked Janus Simulation Centre.

He knocked on the door and introduced himself as Officer Cadet McBride with the artillery. This was still in the early days of JANUS at Gagetown—it had only been set up in March—and people were still learning the ropes.

"Great," said one of the men there. "You can be our artillery, then; come back on the weekend."

Andrew didn't need any more prompting than that. He settled in to a computer station at the back of the room and began learning the system. With Andrew's computer background, he took to it very quickly. On the weekends, when infantry soldiers would arrive to undertake simulated missions, they'd see Andrew there and naturally ask who he was.

"Oh, he's our artillery."

It wasn't long before Andrew became proficient with JANUS and was delivering weekend fire missions whenever called for by the infantry.

Andrew did well that summer on his courses, both in the classroom and out in the field. In fact, he was awarded Top Recce (pronounced *recky* but short for reconnaissance) Patrolman, and LCol J.A.G. Champagne, Commandant of the Infantry School, made a point of personally noting Andrew's performance on the course.

—

Stephan had continued in cadets after Andrew enrolled in ROTP and, like his brother, ended his time as a Warrant Officer. In his last year, he was cadet leader on a tour of Canadian Scottish battlefields through France, Holland and into Germany, retracing the route taken during the Second World War by his grandfather Gorbatuk after whom he was named. That summer, following graduation from high school, Stephan decided to pursue his interest in economics and law. A decade later, he would graduate from Stanford University with a PhD in Economics, having also obtained graduate degrees from Yale University and Queen's University.

—

Andrew's third year at RMC was interrupted briefly, in January, when the Ice Storm of 1998 hit eastern Ontario, southern Québec and parts of New Brunswick. In some places, up to five inches of ice downed power lines, toppled trees, and even collapsed farm buildings. There were thirty-five deaths attributed to the storm which left millions without power—in some cases for as long as a month— during the dead of winter. Both Ottawa and Montréal were crippled. On January 7, Ontario, Québec and New Brunswick called for aid from the Canadian Forces, and Operation Recuperation was launched on January 8. Andrew was one of over 15,000 CF troops to respond, the largest military operation on Canadian soil in response to a natural disaster.

For Kingston and the surrounding townships, the majority of RMC was mobilized, organized as an Army Operational Command, and put in the hands of Army officer cadets—after all, this was the kind of situation that Army officer cadets train for. Andrew was initially appointed a section commander but was almost immediately moved up to Platoon Second in Command and, by the end of the first day, was made the Platoon Commander. Over the next two weeks, as utilities were restored and demand decreased, students started drifting back, but Andrew liked the work and chose to stick around and soon progressed up through the Company and into the Battalion command hierarchy. Eventually he found himself with his own truck and an office at the Emergency Task Force HQ in the fire station even though by then the RMC contingent was fairly small. After it was all over and Operation Recuperation had finally been shut down, Andrew received a commendation from General Maurice Baril who was the Chief of the Defence Staff at the time.

In the spring of 1998, a sparring partner accidentally injured Andrew. It was during a combat drill of some sort. Andrew had his right foot in the air, and his partner's foot landed hard across the top of his. It wasn't intentional or even reckless on the part of his sparring partner; it was just one of those things that can happen in physical situations, the kind of small split-second incident against which there is ultimately no protecting yourself. That one blow, as it turns out, would have unexpected and far-reaching consequences.

At first it wasn't diagnosed as a break, but when it refused to improve, an X-ray showed the truth of matters. The foot is a complicated bit of business, and there was not much to be done short of putting Andrew's lower leg and foot in a cast for a number of months until things set properly. He was in that cast and on crutches for a long time. That was followed by physiotherapy. He was eventually prescribed special orthopaedic boots and was warned by his physiotherapist that injuries to a foot often lead to problems for the opposite knee.

Because of the foot injury, Andrew was unable to go to Gagetown for his BAO III that summer. Instead he stayed in Kingston and worked on his Aikido—while his injury kept him off the mat, there was a great deal of opportunity to work on technique and there were Japanese language commands to master as well.

—

Andrew successfully completed his last year at RMC and, on May 2, 1999, graduated with a BA in Military and Strategic Studies under his belt and was commissioned as a 2nd Lieutenant.

Graduating cadets get to wear the military uniform of their choice at their graduation parade from among those they have been issued. Since Andrew played drums in the RMC pipe band, he chose to wear the kilt with highland headdress. Perhaps the fact that this uniform stood out among the other cadets led the then Minister of Defence, Art Eggleton, to chat him up during inspection.

Though I was unable to be there, Andrew's mother and grandmother flew down to attend his graduation. It was memorable for both, especially for Nana McBride who had attended Andrew's grandfather's wings graduation as an RCAF pilot fifty-eight years earlier.

Andrew was posted to 2nd Regiment, Royal Canadian Horse Artillery in Petawawa as an assistant Gun Positioning Officer but still had to attend the CTC at Gagetown that summer for his BAO III. Just prior to graduation, he'd purchased a red Tercel from someone he knew in Kingston. After graduation, he had most of his effects shipped to Petawawa and drove almost twelve hours to Gagetown. He was twenty-one years old.

That summer, 2Lt McBride spent weekends delivering fire missions on JANUS and successfully completed the third part of his Basic Artillery Officer training. When he was done, he packed what belongings he had with him in New Brunswick and headed west for CFB Petawawa where his career awaited him.

Three

CFB Petawawa has a long history in Ontario. Originally established as a military camp in 1905, on over 22,000 acres (90 square kilometres) in Renfrew County, it was the summer training grounds for A and B Batteries of the Royal Horse Artillery stationed in Kingston. It was the site of the Canada's first military aircraft flight in July of 1909, and during the First World War it served as an internment camp for German prisoners of war. In late 1916, it hosted the Russian artillery for a time. The Russians were considering a purchase of Canadian-made three-inch artillery shells and, after sufficient testing, placed a sizeable order. Unfortunately, before the contract could be fulfilled, the Russian Imperial Government was overthrown. During the Second World War, artillery and engineering training centres were established there and later it served again as an internment camp. Training resumed in 1947, and in 1948, the Royal Canadian Dragoons and 1st Battalion of the Royal Canadian Regiment were moved there. It was made an official permanent camp in 1951 and designated Camp Petawawa. In 1968, Camp Petawawa became CFB Petawawa.

By August of 1999, CFB Petawawa represented more than three hundred square kilometres of the upper Ottawa Valley and Laurentian Hills and was home to the 2nd Canadian Mechanized Brigade Group (2CMBG) which comprises 1st Battalion, The Royal Canadian Regiment; 2nd Battalion, The Royal Canadian

Regiment (stationed at Gagetown); 2 Combat Engineer Regiment; 2nd Regiment, Royal Canadian Horse Artillery; 3rd Battalion, The Royal Canadian Regiment; The Royal Canadian Dragoons; and 2 Service Battalion.

The base motto is in Eastern Anishanaabe rather than latin; it is *Endazhe Kinamandowa Chimaganishak,* which translates to *Training Ground of the Warriors.*

Andrew's posting was to 2nd Regiment, Royal Canadian Horse Artillery (2RCHA) which had three batteries: D, E, and F. Andrew was assigned to D Battery, where his role was assistant Gun Positioning Officer. In the usual course of events, Andrew would have been coming to the posting as a brand new fully qualified artillery officer, but his foot injury meant he was a year behind in his training at Gagetown.

When he first arrived at Petawawa, the Commanding Officer of 2RCHA was Lieutenant-Colonel R.G. Davis, and the Battery Commander for D Battery was Major Brian McPherson. Early on, Andrew spent a lot of time as both Recce Officer and Command Post Officer as need be, and there were occasions— especially later on—when they did not have an actual Gun Positioning Officer and he fulfilled the position regardless of the official title.

To give you a sense of context, here is a rough idea of how an artillery battery works:

In the field, a battery is responsible for six guns, and for D Battery these were M109s—the Canadian Army had purchased 28 GIAT LG1 Howitzers two years earlier, but in August of 1999, only F Battery had them. The M109A4+ is an American-made 155mm self-propelled howitzer. To an untrained civilian these look like tanks, but there is a world of difference between the two. A tank is designed as a front line vehicle. It is heavily armoured and meant to engage directly with enemy forces; its main barrel is not rifled and generally fires line of sight. A self-propelled howitzer is lightly armoured and designed to provide indirect fire support. It has a rifled barrel and is capable of delivering shells up to eighteen kilometres away.

The D Battery M109s could deliver up to six rounds per minute or maintain sustained fire of up to three rounds per minute. They could carry thirty-six rounds, had an operational range of 350 kilometres, and could travel at up to fifty-six kilometres per hour.

Each gun is commanded by a sergeant with seven troops. Each battery also has a Troop Sergeant-Major (TSM) who oversees all three gun detachments. There is also a Troop Commander (or TC, an officer) who relays orders down to the TSM. When in the garrison, the TC reports to the Battery Commander (BC) or his second in command (2IC) the Battery Captain (BK), but in the field, the chain of command running from the guns to the BC is different.

In the field, the Troop Commander reports to the Gun Positioning Officer (GPO). The Battery Commander is fed information from his Forward Observation Officers and relays his orders, based on that information, to the Gun Positioning Officer. It is the GPO who ensures that those orders are executed. The GPO is not only responsible for the operation of the entire gunline but is also in charge of a Reconnaissance Officer (RecceO), who scouts ahead to give assessments for gun movements, and the Command Post Officer (CPO), who is responsible for communication to and from the GPO.

The GPO is usually a senior Lieutenant or junior Captain who has been promoted in the role. Andrew was in a strange position at Petawawa. He was still a Second Lieutenant, and though his superiors recognized his capabilities, his training was behind schedule. This meant that he couldn't yet be permanently assigned as GPO even though that was clearly where he was headed.

And occasionally his lack of training *did* catch up to him. For instance, at one point he located a battery among the trees and was dressed down for it by his Battery Commander Maj McPherson—while trees might offer some visual cover, if they are hit by incoming fire, they can present a host of additional risks. Of course, this was a lesson from BAO IV, and when Andrew had to admit that he'd never been taught that, it caught Maj McPherson off guard.

"Yes, of course, I forget that sometimes. Right, well here's the reasoning…"

In the fall of 1999, a reconnaissance squadron of the Royal Canadian Dragoons was preparing to deploy to Kosovo to relieve the Lord Strathcona Horse (an armoured regiment based out of Edmonton). To prepare them for what they were likely to encounter there, a two-week field exercise was held out of the Land Force Central Area Training Centre in Meaford, Ontario. LCol Davis gave Andrew command of a group of soldiers drawn from 2 Royal Canadian Horse Artillery, the Royal Canadian Dragoons, and the Grey and Simcoe Foresters (the local reserve unit) in order to provide realistic opposing forces.

Operating out of Meaford, they conducted operations across the entire Owen Sound–Orangeville region, approximating the squadron's area of responsibility in Kosovo. Both sides were armed with state-of-the-art weapon effect simulation (WES) systems that accurately registered wounds and kills. Weapons fired blanks and sent out laser pulses that registered on various sensors integrated into the uniforms. Early on, Andrew's direct supervisor was called away on a family emergency; Andrew stepped up and assumed his position as well and found himself answering to the man in charge of the entire exercise, Maj Tim Datchko, the man who would lead the squadron in Kosovo. Datchko gave Andrew a great deal of leeway as he was very interested in "putting the screws" to his men.

Andrew's team embraced the challenge, stepped into the role-playing and really shone over the course of the exercise. When the field exercise was complete, Andrew received a letter of appreciation from the CO of Royal Canadian Dragoon, LCol P.J. Atkinson, who felt that Andrew's team had helped prepare the squadron for what would no doubt be a challenging deployment.

These were the kind of hands-on assignments that Andrew loved. The ones where you had to think on your feet and were expected to get your hands dirty.

One of the properties assigned to 2RCHA on CFB Petawawa was a historical building known as the Russia House, the only remaining structure built to house the delegations from the Czar's Artillery during the First World War. Usually single artillery officers were housed there, but it was at capacity in August of 1999, and so Andrew was billeted in the Officer Quarters with the rest of the Brigade's junior officers for a number of months. He was able to move in to Russia House early in 2000. It would be his home for a number of years.

In May of 2000, he was back at CTC Gagetown, eager to get his BAO IV so he could be finally be assigned as D Battery GPO. His first ten months at CFB Petawawa had been exciting for him, but he was often frustrated by his situation. Andrew was a young man who liked to be at the head of the pack, not lagging behind, and while he realized there was nothing to be done, he wanted to put the delays behind him.

Phase IV of the Basic Artillery Officer course started out with a lot of class work, but that was, as always, offset by a great deal of physical training. That year the PT included a fair amount of running on pavement, and unfortunately this had not *entirely* unforeseen consequences. Andrew had been wearing special orthopaedic boots since injuring his foot at RMC, and although it had been almost two years since he first laced them up, it was likely all the running that year that eventually compromised Andrew's left knee. The physiotherapist had warned that an injury to the right foot often caused problems with the left knee, but Andrew had thought he'd dodged that bullet when he successfully managed to complete BAO III the previous summer.

Andrew had only completed six weeks of the course when he had to be "returned to unit" in late June. At CFB Petawawa he was frustrated and discouraged. The physical training was part of the course—there was no way to avoid that—and this would mean that he would have to try again next year. He would be two years behind schedule and was looking at another year without the proper qualifications needed to assume his role.

Upon returning to Petawawa—in fact when he was in line at the kit exchange—Andrew was approached by a Dragoon whose squad had just returned from Kosovo.

"Sir, I just wanted to thank you for your part in the training operation in Meaford. Your guys really stuck it to us out there."

"It was my pleasure, Trooper." Andrew, I imagine, shot him a slightly evil grin. "I'm glad it helped."

"Y'know at one point in the operation, I was taken, coming around the corner of a house. A chest shot and an outright kill. In fact, five of us were killed in that spot, and it meant us taking a look at the rules of engagement and hashing things out with the officers. Buying it like that, with a Tim Hortons around the corner... well, I gotta tell you, Sir, it sure as hell left an impression on me, and it probably saved my life over there on patrol."

Andrew, a little embarrassed at the praise, took the trooper's hand when he offered it. They shook hands, and then the trooper shot him a salute.

It was not lost on Andrew at that point how even small events can have a big impact down the road. Here he was, returning to Petawawa without his BAO IV due to a knee injury springing from a freak sparring injury in Kingston two years earlier. And at the same time, here was a soldier coming back from Kosovo, crediting a simulated chest wound, something as insubstantial as a pulse of light hitting a sensor, with perhaps saving his life.

Because Andrew had been RTUed in June, it meant that he was back at Petawawa for the arrival of the new 2RCHA regimental commander, LCol John Crosman, LCol Davis having just been promoted to the role of Deputy Base Commander. Andrew had barely spoken to the previous Commander, LCol Davis, and so he was caught off guard when LCol Crosman walked into his office and struck up a conversation. He'd heard that Andrew was a computer whiz and wanted advice on what he should buy and when the next big upgrades were due.

Andrew liked LCol Crosman right away. "A real gunner's gunner," Crosman was highly competent, forward thinking, and detail oriented. He grew up on Army bases throughout Canada and Europe and enrolled the year Andrew was born.

LCol Crosman saw in Andrew a young officer with a lot of promise. He appreciated Andrew's drive and liked his aptitude with technical issues. When the Base Commander unexpectedly tasked Andrew to Ottawa for the summer shortly after LCol Crosman's arrival, Crosman was disappointed to see him go—this was done, however, to "free up a fully qualified officer".

In Ottawa, Andrew was to serve as commander of the exhibition entitled "Army of Tomorrow: Serving You Today" in front of the Canadian War Museum on Sussex. Military vehicles and guns were stationed in the museum courtyard, and the public was invited to explore and ask questions of the personnel manning the display. The director of exhibitions and programmes in charge of the display admitted that she had expected a captain but said that 2Lt McBride comported himself well in the role.

A funny story: At one point, the Armoured Warrant Officer came to Andrew and asked if he should roll the tank; there was a refurbished Leopard C2 as part of the display. It is standard practice not to let military vehicles sit too long on one place, and back at Petawawa, they rolled all the vehicles once a week if they were otherwise stationary. This practice is even more important with tracked vehicles. Andrew thought it a reasonable request and asked if he could ride along.

Andrew rode in the gunner's hatch; there was a Master Corporal in the commander's cupola and a driver in the tank itself. The Warrant Officer was outside on the road. The obvious route took them down Sussex past the National Gallery then right onto Patrick curving behind the Peacekeeping Monument onto Murray and left onto the Sussex and back to the War Museum.

It was the next day that Andrew got a call from a Public Affairs Officer, a captain, telling him to come to HQ on the double. When Andrew arrived he got an earful. The problem is that the route around the Peacekeeping Monument took them directly past the American Embassy, and I guess the security detail at the embassy was made uneasy by the sight of a Leopard C2 tank rolling by unannounced. Needless to say, they didn't roll the tank along that route again.

Upon his return to Petawawa, knee assessment led to surgery in the fall to repair a torn meniscus. This was followed by months of rehab. Nevertheless he pressed forward in Petawawa and grew into his future role as GPO even while waiting to complete the BAO IV course.

He learned how to fire multiple shells from the guns in such a way as to have them land simultaneously, which is now something that is managed by computer. He even attached his own personal computer to the guns at one point and later ran a new computerized fire-control-system for D battery that enabled D Bty to get off its shells and to retrieve and fire the shells E Bty could not get off.

In the spring of 2001, 2RCHA was preparing for deployment to Bosnia, and Headquarters Company was to travel there to make an advance assessment. LCol Crosman wanted Andrew there because, by that time, he considered Andrew his go-to guy. There was one problem, however. Because Andrew had not received his BAO IV the previous year, he would need permission to miss the first two weeks of the course, and the school refused to permit his late arrival. LCol Crosman, a former artillery instructor himself, was surprised and reassured Andrew that he'd sort it out—after all, Andrew had already completed the first six weeks of this course the previous year. Nevertheless, the school remained firm; there would be *no exceptions*, and Andrew would have to attend for course commencement. The CO expressed regret in not having been able to sort it out, and Andrew was unable to accompany him to Bosnia. Andrew was disappointed to have missed the opportunity to help prove himself to LCol Crosman. And so, as required, Andrew attended Gagetown for course commencement in late May.

Four

Andrew's course officer that year was a captain by the name of Dan Bobbitt. Originally from Andrew's regiment, Bobbitt had been transferred to CTC in 1999 and was gone by the time Andrew arrived in August. The scuttlebutt was that the regiment was only too happy to see him go—though obviously that might have been nothing *more* than scuttlebutt. Regardless, Andrew didn't think much of the man the few times he crossed paths with him in 2000 and soon thought less of him once he was his course officer.

In order to become a course officer, Bobbitt would have taken a one-year Instructor in Gunnery course when he first transferred to Gagetown in 1999. In 2000, as a new grad from the course, he would have been assigned to teach recruits to put a little experience under his belt before being allowed to teach junior officers and officer cadets.

In the spring of 2001, Dan Bobbitt was thirty. An officious, by-the-book captain with the air of someone with something to prove, Bobbitt was paired up with an American exchange officer who was, to Andrew's way of thinking, a lot more competent. This would be Bobbitt's first year teaching future artillery officers.

It was a few weeks into the course, the classroom section was just wrapping up, and the senior instructor, Capt Ron MacEachern, stopped by to check in on the fourth-year students, giving them an opportunity to vent without their course officer (Bobbitt) being present. These sort of things always play out more or less the same way, and Andrew has described it as an hour of his life he knew he would never get back. Still, he genuinely liked and respected MacEachern whom he had known for a couple of years at that point. As the session was winding down, the captain mentioned in passing:

"For those of you who know Michelle Knight, she'll be joining you on the course this summer."

There were a few murmurs and some raised eyebrows. Andrew *did* know her, of course; most of them did. Michelle Knight had been a couple years behind him at RMC and had been a subordinate of his on previous courses at Gagetown. The francophone students even had a nickname for her: *bourdon* [bumblebee] because she was forever changing direction. Now, because of Andrew's injuries, she had caught up to him. The talk among other students had been that she was not attending BAO IV because she had opted to take post-graduate work at RMC that summer. Something must have changed.

What struck Andrew most about this news was that Michelle was being allowed to start the course late. Significantly late. He had not been allowed to start late even though, unlike Michelle, he had covered the material the previous year before being returned to unit. LCol Crosman had even tried to intervene on his behalf and had been told that there were to be no exceptions.

After the session, there was to be a break before classes resumed, and Andrew happened to bump into Capt MacEachern in the washroom. His curiosity got the better of him, and he asked the man, as diplomatically as possible, what the deal was with Michelle Knight being allowed to start the course late. The instructor, however, was simply not going to have that conversation and immediately shut him down, telling Andrew not to worry about it. That response told Andrew all he needed to know; sometimes female officers and officer cadets were afforded extra accommodations, especially in the combat arms, in order to help fill gender quotas, for there was pressure from on high to help boost the stats. C'est la vie. Andrew didn't think any more about it.

When class started, Capt Bobbitt stormed in, and he was *furious*. He ordered Andrew out into the hall where he proceeded to chew him out, loud enough for everyone to hear. According to Andrew, Bobbitt was absolutely beside himself and determined to tear as broad a strip off him as possible—all for discreetly asking a question.

He accused Andrew of being presumptuous and incredibly unprofessional and wanted to let him know that he was not going to put up with any more crap like that for the rest of the summer. And that if he caught wind of anything like it again, by God, there were going to be repercussions. And was Andrew absolutely crystal clear on that fact?

Andrew was caught slightly off guard only because Bobbitt's response was so completely over the top. After all, it wasn't like Andrew had raised a big stink and demanded an explanation in front of the other students.

If you ask me, Andrew raising his question was not the only thing Bobbitt was steamed about.

Clearly Capt Bobbitt had some sort of conversation with MacEachern. It is possible that part of that conversation also included—either in detail or broad strokes—the general feeling of Bobbitt's students in terms of how he was running the course thus far. Remember, that was why the senior instructor had dropped in on them in the first place.

The rest of the students on the course were fresh out of RMC, but Andrew was two years into his posting at Petawawa—Bobbitt's old regiment—and the other students would have looked to him as something of a leader. My feeling is that this was Bobbitt's way of sending a message and knocking Andrew down a few pegs.

If Capt Bobbitt was expecting this second lieutenant to be somehow mortified or abashed, he didn't have Andrew's measure at all. Andrew stood there and took it and likely looked at the man like he was a lunatic.

When Bobbitt was done, he ordered Andrew back to class. It's unlikely he improved the opinion of any of his students towards him. As it turns out, 2Lt Michelle Knight never did join them on the course. Instead she transferred out of Artillery altogether and into Intelligence.

A week later, students were slated to do some driving instruction out on range, and when Capt Bobbitt outlined the scope of the training, Andrew had some reservations. Again, he didn't bring them up in front of the other students, but he did voice them to Bobbitt one-on-one outside of the classroom. Again, because Andrew had been at his posting and working D Battery for two years, he did have *some* experience. He had even trained recruits on some of the wheeled vehicles at Petawawa and thought that having students drive the tracked vehicles without being fully familiarized with them first was a waste of time and potentially dangerous. For that reason Andrew felt that he should at the very least voice his concern.

Bobbitt was not receptive.

This training was meant to cover the common artillery vehicles, both wheeled and tracked. The wheeled vehicles included the Iltis (a Volkswagen-made military vehicle similar to a jeep), HLVW (heavy logistics vehicle, wheeled), MLVW (medium logistics vehicle, wheeled), and the LSVW (light support vehicle, wheeled). There was also a tracked vehicle: the M113 armoured personnel carrier.

For the training that day, the students were split into two groups. Andrew's group hit the wheeled vehicles first, and Andrew managed to pass those tests without incident. Tracked vehicles are quite different; these vehicles don't have steering wheels or brakes, only a gas pedal and two lateral torsion bars. When you want to turn in a certain direction, you pull on the corresponding bar, and it slows the tracks on that side of the vehicle.

It was getting later in the day when Andrew and another student were put in an M113A2 Armoured Personnel Carrier. Andrew asked for driving goggles but was told not to worry about it—he was handed ski goggles instead. Andrew was to be the driver; his hatch was on the left side of the vehicle, and the other student was in the crew commander's hatch in the centre of the vehicle. Because it was later in the day and the ski goggles were tinted, Andrew had a hard time seeing where he was going and was relying on his crew commander to keep him on track.

Understand that these are powerful vehicles. The M113A2 boasts a powerful diesel engine, and though it weighs in excess of 11,700 kg, it can achieve a top speed of 67 km/h. Andrew was having a hard time getting the hang of the torsion steering and his "crew commander" wanted him to bleed off some speed. They weren't explicitly told how to brake—you pull both bars back simultaneously—and so they were quickly jockeying left and right bars.

They were coming to the edge of a field with a large swampy area, and the "commander" decided that, to avoid getting bogged down, Andrew should gun it.

Andrew gave it some gas, and seconds later, the M113 hit a small ridge, vaulted upwards, then dropped down into this boggy spot and stopped dead. The other student was thrown free of the vehicle while Andrew was driven face-first into the cupola. His bottom teeth were compressed through his lower lip so hard that they were thrown out of alignment and his top teeth were severely damaged when they hit the metal.

Shaken, the crew commander climbed back into his hatch, and they managed to drive back to the group with Andrew bleeding profusely and in a lot of pain. Andrew got some emergency first aid there, and then a real driver, a non-commissioned member, took one of the LSVWs and evacuated him to the base hospital.

Captain Bobbitt conducted a quick investigation into the incident, and Andrew was asked to give a statement but never heard anything of it again. Andrew's already strained relationship with Capt Bobbitt only soured after that. It was going to be a trying summer.

Andrew found that the long runs on pavement, which had lead to his knee injury, were troublesome with his post-op knee. But he had been cleared to participate in BAO IV, and he knew that the PT was compulsory, so he just soldiered on as best he could. Capt Bobbitt missed no opportunity to chastise Andrew on numerous occasions, going so far as to frame it in a written assessment that Andrew needed to improve his level of physical fitness (no mention of his knee surgery for context). Anyone who knew Andrew, and Bobbitt certainly did, knew that his fitness level was not the issue and that, were it not for his knee injury, he'd be able to run Bobbitt into the ground. Of course, it smacked of petty score settling on Bobbitt's part, but that is the kind of thing that crops up from time to time between two individuals who do not like each other. One simply has to trust that integrity and professionalism ensures that it doesn't actually escalate beyond petty scores.

The final field exercise of the course was a huge undertaking. It was scheduled from July 28 to August 1 and was to be held out in Gagetown's vast 1,100 square kilometre training area. It would bring together not just the artillery students from all the years and their course officers, but also students from the armour, infantry and engineering schools and a large number of recruits needed to fill out the ranks. All told, hundreds of students would test their mettle in a four-day operation that would call upon everything they had learned thus far.

It was during this final field exercise of the training that Andrew's promising career took a hit from which it would, ultimately, never recover. At the time of the incident, Andrew was acting as a Gun Positioning Officer (GPO) a role he had shadowed and occasionally filled in Petawawa for two years.

On the evening of July 30, Andrew conferred with the Gun Line Troop Sergeant Major and decided to set reveille at 0600. After giving those orders, he checked in with the Command Post (CP) to let them know where he would be sleeping and had a brief conversation with the students working there. The CP was manned by two junior students who were taking their Phase III training. One of the students was the acting CPO. What was, in retrospect, most notable about that conversation was that nothing notable was passed to Andrew. Nothing, at the very least, to suggest to Andrew that he should change his reveille time.

Five

On the morning of July 31, Andrew was awoken at 0530 when orders to move arrived at the CP. Andrew rushed to get his team moving, and while he was rushing he was confronted by Capt Bobbitt who asked him if he had received the SITREP suggesting that operations would commence at 0600.

Andrew replied that he had not—knowing full well that, if there has been a SITREP passed to the CPO, it would have come from Capt Bobbitt.

"McBride, what would you do if you were told that the next phase of the operation would commence at 0600?"

"I would waken the battery earlier to ensure that we would be good to go at 0600."

"Were you or were you not given a SITREP regarding the BC and FOOs meeting for orders?"

Andrew remembered the meeting being brought up *in conversation* but nothing that was framed or passed on as a SITREP.

"I was not."

By way of explanation, a SITREP (situation report) is a communication that facilitates troop activities in the field. It provides information as to the current state, but depending on its contents, one might anticipate that some action would follow from it and so prepare accordingly. A SITREP requires that the pro-word 'SITREP' be placed in front of the communication so there will be no misunderstanding or communication breakdowns. Students were taught in the Artillery School to always prefix a SITREP with the pro-word SITREP.

Andrew was not some green officer cadet. He was two years out of RMC and had spent time at Petawawa as the D Battery Gun Positioning Officer. He'd also spent time as a Command Post Officer. None of this was new to him. Nothing that had passed between Andrew and the CPO on the night of July 30 had been prefaced by the word SITREP; furthermore, at no time during the conversation was anything said that made Andrew so much as question his decision to set reveille at 0600.

At the next position (Andrew's team having easily made their time *despite* the late start) Andrew was again approached by Capt Bobbitt and asked if he received the SITREP. In response, Andrew pointed out that though the meeting of the Battery Commanders (BCs) and Forward Obervation Officers (FOOs) was brought up conversationally, it was never clearly or properly framed as a SITREP and furthermore that commencement times were not brought up in a way which made him question his decision to set a 0600 reveille. At that point, Capt Bobbitt told Andrew that he checked with the CPO who claimed to *remember* passing on the SITREP—though he admitted that perhaps it had been passed on as "activities will recommence at 0600".

Hearing this, Andrew wondered why a CPO *wouldn't* have used the word SITREP and, more conspicuously, why Bobbitt didn't seem to have a problem with that in this instance. While acting as D Battery CPO, Andrew had never once passed on a SITREP without properly framing it as such, nor had any D Battery CPO ever passed SITREP to him so sloppily. It just wasn't done that way, and Bobbitt knew that.

Andrew insisted that nothing anywhere near that clear had been passed on to him—otherwise he would have acted. Capt Bobbitt then said that he *knew* Andrew was lying (which is ridiculous because he could not know what he did not witness, but it is the kind of statement that someone of rank can make with impunity). What was more likely, of course, is that the CPO was saving his own skin by reframing the clarity of the conversation after the fact.

Andrew vigorously objected and pointed out that it would make no sense to have been given that information in any recognizable fashion and voluntarily chosen to ignore it, putting himself in jeopardy. Though the CPO might try to get himself *out* of trouble after the fact (he did not suggest this).

Capt Bobbitt left and returned later to inform Andrew that he had to attend a Progress Review Board (PRB) hearing to review the SITREP. Andrew was then made to sign an Incident Report which read: *As GPO failed to demonstrate integrity and take responsibility for not acting on a SITREP passed to him by the CPO. Instead he lied and stated that he had not received the SITREP from the CPO.* Andrew signed the report and noted "Does Not Agree."

Because the final exercise was taking place deep in the training area, the Progress Review Board hearings were not being held at the base proper but rather in a range hut out on the training grounds. Lawfield Observation Post is located at the southeastern border of the artillery range at the edge of what is known as the Lawfield Impact. It is about twenty-two kilometres southeast of Gagetown's main gate, effectively in the middle of nowhere.

En route to the range hut, Andrew twice asked Capt Bobbitt to bring the two other students as witnesses to the hearing—which would only make sense considering the nature of the disagreement—but was told that he couldn't as the hearing was administrative, not disciplinary. It seemed an odd request to deny, unless of course the witnesses might not back up Bobbitt's version of events.

Due to the scale of the exercise, Andrew knew that his would not be the only PRB being convened, and sure enough, upon arrival he found that there were hearings being held for many soldiers—more than he would have guessed. There was no indication when his hearing would come up, so he took the time to collect his thoughts and write some notes in his field notebook.

There was something not right about this, and Bobbitt's animosity towards him made him edgy. Andrew was exhausted. Sleep deprivation was an integral part of the exercise, and everyone involved was working through some level of sleep debt. When he was done writing his notes, he lay down on the ground to get some rest.

As it turned out, proceedings for the day wrapped up without Andrew's case coming up. He was, therefore, transported back to the guns and went back to work (which entailed being up all night). The next day he was again transported to the range hut where, again, he grabbed some more sleep. The hearing was finally convened at 1530, Wednesday August 1, 2001.

The board comprised LCol K.F. Haeck as chairman, Maj J.G.E. Tremblay as deputy chairman—Tremblay was also Haeck's deputy CO at the artillery school—plus six board members, including Captains MacEachern and Bobbitt. The initial discussion of the board occurred without Andrew in attendance. When that was complete, he was marched in. LCol Haeck briefed him on the nature and reason for the hearing and gave Andrew a synopsis of what Capt Bobbitt had told the board. He then closed his remarks by suggesting that the PRB was to address Andrew's difficulty with ethical decisions. Andrew was then asked if he had anything to add or if he agreed with the synopsis.

A little shaken at that point, Andrew stated that he did not agree with the interpretation that he had lied. He did not believe that a SITREP had been clearly passed to him. He admitted, however, that stress and sleep deprivation may have played a factor. He went on to say that he believed he was an asset to 2RCHA, that he loved his job, thought he was good at it, and wished only to continue.

Andrew was then asked to leave while the board discussed the matter again. There was, perhaps, more Andrew might have said, but he was an exhausted twenty-four-year-old second lieutenant standing up, without representation, in front of a lieutenant-colonel, three majors, three captains and a chief warrant officer. He was a little shell-shocked.

When he was brought back in, he was told by LCol Haeck that a decision would be rendered on Monday August 6. He was then dismissed and driven back out to the guns to finish up the exercise. It was odd for someone to come back from a PRB without a decision. The night before was different; Andrew's case hadn't been heard. But no one had ever heard of someone coming back from a PRB with a pending decision. Usually those students hauled off were either cleared or failed—if they were failed they were not seen again. One possible explanation is that his disappearance the previous day had so impacted his entire team in terms of successfully completing the exercise that the decision was put off until Monday. Of course that explanation assumes that LCol Haeck knew he was going to fail Andrew already.

—

I arrived the next day. It was then, on the way from the airport to the base, that Andrew pulled off the road and told me what had happened. When I heard the story Andrew had to tell, you could say that I had a lot of reservations about how the hearing had progressed.

I told Andrew that, no matter which way LCol Haeck ruled, things were far from over. That there were serious flaws in what had happened and that, if things went against him, we would definitely appeal.

The barbecue was a private affair held at the residence of one of the course instructors; it was a celebration for the senior students completing the Basic Artillery Officer course. It had been an intense summer, and the final exercise had been gruelling. For most of these students, they would be off to their posting to start their careers in less than a week. Andrew's mood was somewhat dark. The best case scenario was that he would likely have to repeat the course next year.

Another year lost—and that was the best case scenario. Though it wasn't mentioned in the hearing, failing training for ethical issues might be the end of his career. Of course, his classmates all knew what was going on, and they sympathized. This was a group of young men and women who were looking forward to the horizon and what lay beyond it. I got the sense that they were all grateful to have dodged the kind of stray bullet that had struck Andrew.

As planned, I stayed at the barracks that night. I doubted that I would be staying there until the graduation ceremony, but I would need to stay until Monday when Andrew received the ruling from LCol Haeck.

Friday was spent by the students cleaning up stores and kit for return to the quartermaster. There were weapons checks as well. Everything needed to be accounted for and put in its place for next year's students.

The next day, Andrew and I drove to Moncton to visit with some family I had there. Though we had a good visit, I could feel Andrew's preoccupation.

I saw Andrew briefly on Monday morning before he went to see LCol Haeck. He looked grim, and I reminded him that, regardless of the ruling, things were not over. There were grievance processes available to him, and the case against him was weak. I told him to stay calm, to wait see what Haeck had to say and that we would go from there.

Shortly after Andrew left, a young helmeted captain walked into the barracks looking for 2Lt McBride. He didn't introduce himself and neither did I. Something in his demeanour struck me as uncomfortable. When he asked, I told him that Andrew had gone to see the CO. I can't recall if he thanked me. That would be the one and only time I ever laid eyes on Capt Dan Bobbitt.

When Andrew presented himself to LCol Haeck on the morning of August 6, the school commandant told Andrew that he was terminating his training, awarding course failure and would, furthermore, be recommending release from the Canadian Forces. Andrew was stunned. This man had just told him that the life he had planned to lead was not going to happen. What else was said I am not sure. If there was any sort of exchange been Andrew and Haeck, he didn't share it with me. When he came back to the barracks he looked like someone who'd been punched in the gut and had not yet caught his breath.

I was angry on my son's behalf but knew that my role was to keep him focused on the next step of the process, one where I could play an active role. Andrew had been told to come back that afternoon for the minutes of the PRB and his course report. It was the Monday of the August long weekend and Armed Forces Day at CFB Gagetown, a day when the base was opened to the public. There would also be demonstrations and a military parade in Fredericton. Rather than brooding, I suggested that we take in some of the events.

The parade in Fredericton included a Leopard tank similar to the one Andrew had ridden past the American Embassy, and I was about to make some sort of comment when Andrew received a call on his cell. It was from CFB Petawawa. LCol Crosman. The news had obviously reached him and he wanted to hear Andrew's side of things. When he did he was absolutely incredulous.

"Christ, that's just the fog of war. This sort of thing happens all the time. When you get back to base, we'll work on a grievance."

When Andrew showed up that afternoon he was told to report back the following morning. When he showed up on the morning of the August 7, he was told to report back that afternoon; that afternoon he was told to report back again in the morning. Andrew was fuming by this point, and I couldn't blame him. LCol Haeck had told Andrew that he was going to flunk him from the course and have him released from Canadian Forces and then put him off three times waiting for the paperwork he'd need to mount a proper grievance.

Andrew just wanted to get back to Petawawa and forego the paperwork.

"They can send it there. This is *bullshit.*"

But my instincts told me that'd be a mistake. We needed that paperwork as a starting point, and the delays might creep or blossom into something else if he didn't bother to pick them up in person. We came very close to having a full-blown falling out over this point. And I knew that if the paperwork wasn't there for Andrew the next morning there'd be a second round.

I was a long time getting to sleep that night in the barracks. I couldn't figure out what was going on. The minutes of a meeting are taken at the meeting—or are supposed to be—so how long does it take to get them typed out? The course report is a series of assessments awarded over the summer as the course progressed. What was taking so long? Was LCol Haeck (or his immediate staff) simply incompetent, or was he being a prick and playing with Andrew? I suppose it could have been a combination of the two. Or perhaps there was a glimmer, even then, that there was a problem with the decision and Haeck was giving the minutes some extra attention. What was said to LCol Crosman, and by whom? What was Crosman's response? Maybe there was a sense that this was going to come back on him. Who knows? It's all speculative at this point.

On the morning of August 8, Andrew went back to LCol Haeck one last time. He received the minutes of his PRB and his course report and signed for them. We loaded up Andrew's car and headed west for Petawawa. It would be a twelve-hour drive, and as we crossed the iron bridge over the Oromocto river, Andrew's course mates back at Gagetown were getting ready for their graduation.

Interlude

Back at Petawawa, Andrew was immediately back to his duties. Both LCol Crosman and I felt confident that a thorough grievance would set things right. The first draft of the grievance was dated August 10, and I would spend much of the next two months back in Nanaimo making sure everything was set out clearly and unequivocally.

I had studied the minutes from the PRB and gleaned what I could from them. It's odd: the board consisted of LCol Haeck (Cmdt), Maj Tremblay (DCmdt), Maj Keffer (CSO), Maj Williams (CIG), Capt MacEachern (SI Fd), Capt Bobbitt (Crse Offr), CWO Jordan (RSM), and Capt Hogan (Adjt). After Andrew was asked to leave the hearing, LCol Haeck put four options to the board members. Andrew could be deemed to have completed the course; he could be deemed to have failed the course and need to retake it the following year; he could be retained for another trade (i.e., not artillery); he could be recommended for release altogether.

The votes were entered not by name but by role. All three majors recommended that Andrew be failed from the course and allowed to take it again the following year. Two of the captains, namely the Crse Offr (Bobbitt) and the SI Fd (MacEachern) voted that he be released. This left Capt Hogan (Adjt) and Chief Warrant Officer Jordan (RSM), but neither of *their* votes are mentioned anywhere in the minutes. What is odd is that there is a recommendation for release from an unnamed Standards Officer (Stds O) who is not mentioned as one of the board members present. Also, the SI Fd vote is mentioned twice, and so, at a glance, it looks like four votes for release versus three for recourse.

What were the recommendations from the Adjutant, Capt Hogan, and the Regimental Sergeant Major, CWO Jordan? Impossible to say. Who was this unnamed Standards Officer mentioned nowhere else in the minutes? It was all pretty fishy.

Of course, LCol Haeck was free to find as he saw fit regardless of recommendations from the board. But the more I thought about the delays in surrendering the minutes to Andrew, the more I felt convinced that the books had been cooked somehow in the interim.

The problem we faced was that, while we had to fight for Andrew, we couldn't fight in a way that might compromise his future. LCol Haeck would still be the Commandant of the Artillery School if Andrew was allowed back the next year, and more to the point, Capt Bobbitt would still be a course officer. While Capt Bobbitt could be as prejudicial with his opinions of Andrew as he liked, if it ever came down to it, we would have to tread lightly with our opinions and speculations when it came to Capt Bobbitt. While there was still a lot to say in our grievance, there was also a lot we could not say.

I know that for Andrew, though it was good that he was back to work, it must have felt as though a long shadow had followed him from Gagetown. Life at Petawawa moved forward regardless.

In September, it was proposed that senior officers in the regiment should get some experience with war gaming, and Major R. Farrell approached Andrew to see if he could help out. He was a natural choice, and he was pleased to get the opportunity. In the event there was, shall we say, some reluctance to having a junior 2nd lieutenant instructing the more senior experienced officers.

On the morning of September 11, Andrew was participating in a combat simulation session when news reached them that American Airlines Flight 11 had crashed into the North Tower of the World Trade Centre. Of course, participants were incredulous that such an accident could happen today. When word came that a second plane,

United Airlines Flight 93, had crashed into the South Tower, it was clear to everyone that America was under attack. The session was terminated and everyone reported back to their units.

At the time, D Battery was designated the Disaster Assistance Response Team unit, and Andrew was involved with its defence and security detail. DART was immediately activated and prepped to leave. As a back-up officer, Andrew would not normally have expected to go initially, but not all members of the unit would arrive for an imminent departure, and so Andrew requested permission to go. Permission was granted so long as Andrew could make departure. Andrew lived three minutes away; he raced to the Russia House, grabbed his go-kit and returned to get on the bus.

As it turned out, departure was delayed bit by bit and eventually cancelled. However, the trajectories of both the Canadian and American militaries were fundamentally altered that day.

Part 2:
The Fog of War

Six

Canada's military is a monolithic organization. Powerful, hierarchical, and intractable by nature, the Canadian Forces is similar to the militaries all over the world in this respect. It is an environment predicated on authority and the willingness of its members to follow orders.

So what do you do when you find yourself at odds with decisions affecting you? It can be a daunting prospect, considering that individual members of the Canadian Forces are not represented in the same way that an employee with a large union might be. There is, however, a grievance process in place.

Section 29 of the *National Defence Act* states:

> "An officer or non-commissioned member who has been aggrieved by any decision, act or omission in the administration of the affairs of the Canadian Forces for which no other process for redress is provided under this Act is entitled to submit a grievance."

Andrew had been aggrieved, and his military career was in jeopardy as a result. Though I was a lawyer by trade and able to articulate the issues at play, it certainly would not have taken a lawyer to see that *something* was not right. Here was a junior officer whose future with the Canadian Forces being compromised based almost entirely on the highly subjective accusation of another officer (only slightly less junior) with whom he had a brief but contentious history.

Of course, a Progress Review Board heard the case, and the matter at hand was considered by a number of higher-ranking officers, including three majors and the commanding officer of the school itself, LCol K.F. Haeck. Some among you might be thinking that the accusation, therefore, was given due consideration and that Andrew ought to have simply accepted the ruling.

But it wasn't that straightforward.

This needs to be made clear up front. My primary involvement with Andrew's case was not based on the *ruling* of the Progress Review Board. My primary concern and the basis for the grievance was the way Andrew's case was handled. From a procedural standpoint, what took place in the Lawfield OP range hut on the afternoon of August 1 was fundamentally unsound, and a basic legal tenet is that a verdict that flows from a trial or hearing which is procedurally unsound cannot be considered valid. It doesn't mean that the verdict is wrong (though in this case I certainly felt it was) only that it is not valid. To arrive at a valid verdict, the case must be tried in a way that is procedurally sound. Without the underpinnings of procedural fairness, the entire legal system falls apart.

First of all, Andrew was not given ample time or opportunity to prepare and present a case. He was denied access to witnesses and was not presented, in a timely or meaningful way, with the evidence against him. Furthermore, Capt Bobbitt, his accuser, was able to apply undue influence over the decision-maker having a seat on the board and access to the decision-maker (Haeck) before, during, and after Andrew's extremely limited participation in the hearing itself.

But all of that is small potatoes compared to the most glaring issue: Evidence.

There is a long-established rule of evidence stating that indirect or *hearsay* evidence cannot be preferred (which is to say accepted) over contradictory direct evidence.

Capt Bobbitt was present for his own initial conversation with the Command Post Officer, but he was not present for the Command Post Officer's subsequent conversation with Andrew. The only people present at that conversation were Andrew and the two students manning the command post—and Bobbitt had conspicuously not allowed *their* testimony even though Andrew had requested it twice.

On the morning of July 31, Capt Bobbitt confronted Andrew about receiving a SITREP the night before, and when Andrew denied having received one, Capt Bobbitt went to talk to the students at the Command Post. At the next opportunity Capt Bobbitt came back and accused Andrew of lying—in fact he claimed that he *knew* Andrew was lying—and it was that accusation which triggered the Progress Review Board hearing.

The fundamental problem is that no one on the board ever heard a *single word of direct evidence* to back up that accusation. They only heard Capt Bobbitt's *version* of the evidence. Had Andrew been asked in a direct and meaningful way, he might have provided direct evidence of the conversation in question. Capt Bobbitt's version was hearsay evidence, which is to say second-hand or indirect evidence. Neither LCol Haeck nor the board members nor Andrew knows verbatim what was asked of the students on the morning of July 31—students who reported to Capt Bobbitt, it should be noted. Neither LCol Haeck nor the board members nor Andrew knows verbatim the responses they gave. The entire case against Andrew was presented and characterized second-hand by his accuser. It does not take a great legal mind to recognize that this is problematic.

Then there is the matter of the burden of proof. As the individual levelling the accusation, Capt Bobbitt had the burden of proof set squarely on his shoulders. It was not up to Andrew to prove that he hadn't lied, it was up to Capt Bobbitt to prove that he had. And in a case like this, the standard of proof must be considered high indeed.

Not only was a young man's career at stake, but the accusation itself was highly subjective.

Consider this: the accusation was not that Andrew failed to set the correct reveille time (that would have been easily proved and more or less objective). The accusation was not even that Andrew ought to have known to set the correct reveille time (that would have been a subjective call speaking to his competence rather than his integrity). The actual accusation brought against Andrew was that he had lied as to whether he ought to have known to set the correct reveille time.

Without hearing a single syllable of direct evidence from the conversation in question, the assembled board (which included the accuser) was being asked to rule on whether Andrew had lied about what he had been told.

During Andrew's time at CFB Petawawa, he had served as the acting Gun Positioning Officer on a number of occasions. He had also served, at various times, as the D Battery Command Post Officer. He was an experienced, highly-motivated individual looking to finally complete his training which had twice been delayed.

Even a fleeting nod to common sense would tell you that no credible narrative exists where Andrew receives a clear indication that reveille ought to be moved forward and chooses not to do so. The only reasonable assumption is that, if he left the command post thinking that 0600 was the correct time for reveille, it was because he had received no compelling indication to the contrary.

In short, the Progress Review Board hearing of August 1 was fatally flawed. That LCol Haeck somehow failed to recognize it as such was unconscionable. While I cannot speak to LCol Haeck's qualifications and capabilities as an officer, I can say that his legal judgement was, in this instance, slipshod at best.

All of this (minus my opinion of LCol Haeck's legal acumen) was included in Andrew's PRB grievance which we completed and filed on October 24, 2001.

Here's how the grievance process is *supposed* to work: The PRB grievance is sent to the grievor's commanding officer who then forwards it to the appropriate commander. In this case, the grievance was sent to LCol John Crosman, the CO of the 2nd Regiment, Royal Canadian Horse Artillery in Petawawa, and he forwarded it to LCol K.F. Haeck, the commander of the Artillery School at Gagetown.

If the commander receiving the grievance is *not* the individual who rendered the initial decision, then he, as Initial Authority (IA), has sixty days to respond. Otherwise, as was the case here, he has ten days to forward it to an *appropriate* IA, usually the next person in the chain of command, in this case Colonel Michael Ward, the Commander of the Combat Training Centre. Furthermore, any documents or correspondence reviewed by the IA must be disclosed to the member seeking redress.

All of this is pretty sensible and straightforward. An individual says, *I don't agree with this decision against me,* and outlines his reasons, which are then sent through the chain of command so that someone else can give it a second look. That's the theory. However, in retrospect, I am reminded of something the inimitable Yogi Berra once said.

> "In theory, there's no difference between theory
> and practice, but in practice, there is."

Meanwhile, back at CFB Petawawa, while I had been working on the grievance, 2RCHA was possibly being re-rolled as infantry for overseas deployment. This involved extensive training in infantry tactics and numerous dismounted patrols were planned. For various reasons, Andrew went out with them on seven of the scheduled patrols. Before the eighth one, LCol Crosman pulled him aside and told Andrew that, while his dedication and commitment were appreciated, he had to be careful not to show up the other officers, cancelling his planned participation.

However, one additional patrol was scheduled, this time an assault boat river crossing, and Andrew was *selected* to lead it. It was considered a difficult field exercise. Andrew asked around how one goes about a river crossing, but no one at the regiment had experienced one.

Now one of Andrew's field practices came into play. Since D Battery was mechanized—meaning it used motorized transport—he always took his computer, cot and books whenever he went into the field. Fortunately one those books actually covered conducting an assault boat river crossing and, under Andrew's command, the patrol succeeded in conducting one.

On November 7, we received a written acknowledgement from LCol Haeck stating that he had received the grievance. It was now, for the time being, out of our hands.

Truth be told, Andrew was pretty upset at this point, and part of the reason he was throwing himself into the field exercises was to take his mind off what has happening. He was twenty-four years old, and his life, since he was twelve, had been all about pursuing a career in Canadian Forces; now all of that had been jeopardized with an accusation by one individual with a chip on his shoulder—though the fault for the farcical hearing has to rest on LCol Haeck's shoulders, not Bobbitt's.

I suppose I should make it clear that no one was questioning CF's authority to render a judgement on Andrew. You simply don't pursue a military career if you have a problem with authority—and Andrew certainly had none. In effect, all we were suggesting was that, if it was not too much trouble, the exercising of that authority be at the very least procedurally fair.

As it would turn out, that was asking far too much.

Seven

It was mid-January when I received a phone call from Andrew that sorely, if briefly, tested our working relationship. I could tell by the tone of his voice that it wasn't good news. In retrospect, I didn't field things as well as I might have, but the problem was that what he was about to tell me didn't add up.

"I heard back from Haeck. He's turned us down. It's like he didn't even read it."

"Wait. Who was the initial authority?"

"Haeck."

"No, Haeck rendered the ruling, he had to send it to someone else for review."

"It was Haeck."

"Son, he *can't* review his own decision. Apart from being pointless, he's prohibited from doing so."

"Well, he did."

"No. Look, he's simply not—"

"Lieutenant Colonel K.F. Haeck, Commandant of the Artillery School. What do you want me to tell you, Dad? I learned to read in grade school, remember?" Andrew was clearly annoyed, and I wasn't helping matters any.

I took a deep breath.

"All right. Okay. Why don't you just tell me what it says."

The response was dated December 21, and of course, Andrew had it right. LCol Haeck *had* acted as Initial Authority, despite specific prohibitions barring him from doing so, and reviewed his own decision. It took the man forty-four days to let us know that he was deciding to agree with himself. There had been no disclosure during that time because he had not reviewed any new information.

In effect, LCol Haeck had decided that, although there was an established CF protocol for grievances in matters such as this, Andrew was not entitled to it. LCol Haeck had reviewed the PRB findings and his decision to end Andrew's training and recommend his release from CF and decided that everything was in order. He did not address a single issue brought up in the grievance as to the procedural inadequacies of the hearing itself.

His one notable contribution to the process made even less sense than his failure to follow proper protocol, and suggests a man who was either not giving the matter his full attention or was simply unable to comprehend the fundamental underpinnings of the grievance itself.

In his response, LCol Haeck actually provided an explanation for events which did not involve Andrew lying. He stated that the pro-word SITREP was *deliberately* not used by the CPO as part of a test to see if Andrew would pick up on the fact that he had been passed a SITREP. Apart from the fact that there was not so much as a whiff of this during the initial PRB hearing and there was no disclosure to suggest any new information was reviewed, this completely undermined the very decision he was choosing to uphold.

To suggest that the CPO had *deliberately* tested Andrew—assumedly under the instruction of Capt Bobbitt—by not using the pro-word SITREP introduces the possibility of Andrew not realizing that he'd been passed a SITREP at all, which in turn *precludes* him lying about it. If Capt Bobbitt had *instructed* this junior student to *deliberately* circumvent established protocol, how clear were his instructions? And how effectively did said student manage to interpret and improvisationally carry out those instructions? These questions were at the absolute core of the case, but no satisfactory answers existed because not a single word of direct testimony was ever heard.

So, to review:

Here we had a lieutenant-colonel who had entertained a hopelessly flawed PRB hearing that contained not a shred of direct evidence supporting the accusation. He ruled that Andrew was to be awarded a course failure and thrown out of CF *for lying*. He later reviews his own ruling, contrary to regulations barring him from doing so, does not address the actual concerns of the grievance in front of him, upholds his original ruling, and at the same time offers an explanation which suggests that Andrew did not lie at all.

I ask you, what is a rational individual to take from all that?

The grievance process allows the aggrieved party to file a grievance if they have cause not to agree with the response of the Initial Authority. This is important because the Initial Authority is often directly responsible for the individual who passed the original ruling, and a possibility exists that they are not going to be wholly objective. Of course, in the case of Andrew's grievance it didn't even reach the proper Initial Authority—in this case it would have been Col Ward the Commander of the Combat Training Centre—because LCol Haeck decided to review his own ruling.

A grievance filed against an Initial Authority response is sent to a Final Authority, and in the case of an officer facing release from the Canadian Forces, the Final Authority is always the Chief of the Defence Staff. We began work on a second grievance which would reiterate all the issues articulated in the first grievance in terms of procedural inadequacies and lack of evidence. We would then build on that by pointing out that LCol Haeck had demonstrated further disregard for process by acting as his own Initial Authority and having failed to provide any disclosure, even though there were new aspects brought into the case, i.e., the fact that the pro-word SITREP had been omitted.

Andrew's former Battery Commander, Maj McPherson, had gone to RMC in the fall to pursue a degree in Military Arts and Sciences and was replaced by a Maj Morrison. Morrison's second in command was a Battery Captain by the name of Steve Hunter. It was near the end of March 2002, while I was still finalizing the revised grievance, that Captain Hunter dropped a bombshell on Andrew.

They were talking in Hunter's office about future plans for the battery when, in a moment of candour, the conversation shifted and Andrew was broadsided.

"Look McBride, I want to be honest with you. I don't know the state of your grievances, and it's not my business to know, but between you and me, the word has already come down from NDHQ that you're being released. That is my business, especially when it comes to planning because it puts the battery in a complicated situation."

Andrew felt the ground shift beneath his feet. We were still pursuing a grievance against the flimsy PRB ruling that was set to *recommend* release. For Andrew to be released, that recommendation would first need to trigger an actual Administrative Review. If an Administrative Review determined that Andrew should be released, there would be grievance opportunities at that point as well— unless, of course, it had all been decided already and the process was just a dog and pony show.

Andrew was shaken after he left his meeting with Captain Hunter. It'd been almost eight months since his career had unexpectedly gone off the rails. The grievance process was not working the way it was supposed to, and he felt that things were happening behind the scenes to force him out. He felt anxious and distracted.

His demeanour didn't go unnoticed for long and soon he found himself talking to the regimental medical officer, a captain whom I never met—indeed I didn't hear about this incident at the time. Andrew explained his situation to the doctor with growing frustration. She prescribed a stress leave and Andrew agreed. For the next ten days, though Andrew stayed on the base, he was not expected to attend to any duties. He did a lot of soul searching and tried to get his head screwed on right. Part of the problem was that he didn't have a backup plan. While he was a bright, highly-capable young man, his long-term plan for as long as he'd had one had been a career in the Canadian Forces. He didn't want to give up on that.

Andrew was still on stress leave when, on April 3, we filed an amended grievance which reiterated the concerns in the initial grievance and included numerous issues brought up with LCol Haeck's mishandling of the response. We requested at that time that it be sent to General Henault, the Chief of the Defence Staff as Final Authority for adjudication. I sent it to CFB Petawawa for Andrew's signature and from there it was given to LCol Crosman.

On May 22, LCol Crosman received a letter from the office of the Director of the Canadian Forces Grievance Authority (DCFGA). It stated that, as LCol Haeck had not been the correct IA, it would be sent instead to Colonel Ward, the Commander of the Combat Training Centre, who would act as the proper IA. Colonel Ward had been CCed on the letter.

We weren't too happy with that news. What it meant was that LCol Haeck—whether through sheer incompetence or by design— had effectively wasted seven months in the process. And Andrew was all too aware, since his conversation with Capt Hunter, that the clock was ticking.

We got a call from Andrew near the end of the month. It was after dinner in Nanaimo, meaning it must have been quite late there in Petawawa. Kerry picked up, and she and Andrew spoke for a few minutes before she handed the phone to me. With her hand over the receiver she mouthed the words *he sounds upset.*

I don't know if something else had happened that day or if the stress was simply catching up to him, but he sounded a little grim. He was questioning whether he should just throw in the towel; this was never something I'd heard from Andrew.

"Andrew, I know this has been hard for you, but there is a process in place. We have a strong case. Who knows, perhaps it's just Haeck. Maybe Ward looks at it and decides to deal with it properly rather than see it land on General Henault's desk."

"It's just…well, it's awkward here because I'm in limbo. Not having the qualifications is complicating things on this end for everyone. It's demoralizing, and after what Capt Hunter said, I don't know, maybe this is just a waste of time."

"It's your call, Andrew. But I think you should trust in the process. We're not out of options yet by a long shot."

There was a long pause on the other end of the line.

"Yeah, okay. I suppose you're right."

Eight

June passed without a response from Col Ward, and it was hard to judge whether that boded well or ill for Andrew, but there was nothing to do but wait. Then in July, the landscape changed. Word began to spread that there was going to be another change of command in the regiment. LCol Crosman, who had for two years been in Andrew's corner, was moving on to his next assignment and his replacement was to be a Lieutenant-Colonel Kevin Cotten who was coming to 2RCHA from Land Forces Western Area Headquarters.

Soon after LCol Cotten took command of the regiment, the word *release* appeared beside Andrew's name on the posted officer slate. He had already been pulled from D Battery and assigned to a desk in regimental headquarters. Andrew was devastated; he lived for the rigours and challenges of field.

His own troops, guys he had formed close working relationships with, were now asking him when his release date was and what his plans were once he got out—as though it were a voluntary release. He didn't know what to tell them. The Army was acting as if his release were a done deal, but there hadn't even been an Administrative Review scheduled to *consider* his release yet.

He was being deliberately marginalized. Railroaded.

It was the end of August before we heard anything back from Colonel Ward. That was, of course, beyond the allowed response time, but that was easily circumvented by simply *dating* the response as having been made on July 31, 2002. There was no explanation as to why it would take a month to hear the results of the decision, but we had to pick our battles.

According to the official date on the document it was exactly one year to the day after Capt Dan Bobbitt felt compelled to accuse Andrew of lying that Colonel Ward delivered his IA response. In it we see the careful footwork of a man determined to avoid the issue entirely. "The dilemma," he wrote in his response, "is did you or did you not lie."

While that was indeed the *original dilemma,* it was categorically *not* the issue of the grievance in front of him. The nature of a grievance in front of Col Ward (and LCol Haeck before him) was that the ruling could not be reasonably made because the hearing *itself* was fundamentally deficient and that, furthermore, it did not meet the standard of proof required to reasonably pass the judgement arrived upon. For Col Ward to frame the issue in front of him as whether Andrew lied was to be blind to the basic facts which constituted the grievance itself.

Col Ward did not hold a new hearing, which even a year later would have been the obvious course of action; instead he chose to review the written record and ignore the fact that it was predicated entirely on hearsay evidence and thus fundamentally flawed. How he decided that one-year-old hearsay evidence was somehow no longer hearsay is beyond me. That done, he simply chose to accept the PRB's findings. Like LCol Haeck before him, however, he added an alternative explanation to Andrew lying to Capt Bobbitt.

It is in the field, Col Ward wrote, *under changing and demanding conditions, that the true test is being conducted.* Yes, the military even has a term for foul-ups, referring to them as resulting from the "fog of war". Perhaps a junior course officer might not have experience with activities in the field not always going according to plan, but senior officers certainly would. Indeed, there is a second military expression used to describe this reality: SNAFU.

In other words, an officer more seasoned than Captain Bobbitt (someone like the Colonel himself one assumes) might have recognized this incident for what it actually was—a communication breakdown attributable, at least in part, to sleep debt and in this case a *deliberate* deviation from standard protocol.

The problem of course is that, despite the sage Colonel's apparent understanding of the *fog of war*, he decided, for reasons known only to himself, to rule that Andrew had not been a victim of it and had instead outright lied. Andrew was facing a release process that had already seen him removed from the guns and would get no help from the Commander of the Combat Training Centre where this SNAFU had taken place.

It is worth pointing out that the Commander had taken the helm at the CTC a year before, the same month that Andrew had inadvertently run afoul of Capt Bobbitt for the last time. Though a relative newcomer to this particular post, every single act of this Kafkaesque drama to that point took place under his watch.

As a full Colonel, we must give Michael Ward the benefit of the doubt for being neither incompetent nor simpleminded. Unfortunately that doesn't leave him a great deal of wiggle room in terms of explanations when it comes to his decision. One can only assume that he was being deliberately obtuse and choosing to ignore the fundamental issues with the original PRB and/or being unofficially complicit with a general feeling that Andrew's case had generated sufficient bad blood that Andrew needed to go, regardless of protocol.

Of course, it's also worth pointing out that July of 2002 saw the promotion of LCol Haeck to the position of Col Ward's Chief of Staff. Considering that the amended grievance had pointed out the egregious shortcomings of LCol Haeck's original hearing and Haeck's inappropriate decision to subsequently review his own grievance, one can't help but wonder if Col Ward was faced with a decision as to who would be tossed under the bus—his new Chief of Staff, or some unfortunate second lieutenant he barely knew.

Either way, one would think that, after a full year as the Commander of the Combat Training Centre, Col Ward would have had time to take the Gagetown motto to heart. That motto is, after all, pretty simple. It is one word.

Diligence.

When we got Col Ward's response, I let Andrew know that we should see things through and send an amended grievance to the Chief of the Defence Staff for final adjudication. Pulling Andrew from the guns had been a move aimed at disheartening him in hopes that he would give up the fight. The fact of the matter was that the two responses we'd received thus far were notably weak. I pointed out that the benefit of having the CDS as final authority is that all grievances directed there were first sent to the Canadian Forces Grievance Board for assessment. The grievance board does most of the legwork, reviewing the grievance. It is supposed to disclose all material it plans to consider and solicit feedback during the disclosure process. The CFGB then makes its *recommendations* for the CDS. Effectively they brief the CDS as to what his response ought to be based on their findings. These folks would be forced to address the grievance seriously.

Neither LCol Haeck nor Col Ward—nor whoever was pulling strings at National Defence Headquarters in Ottawa—wanted to see this grievance reach the CFGB. But we had nothing to lose. Andrew hadn't been released yet, despite the petty theatrics suggesting otherwise.

Regimental Headquarters did not really need an assistant adjutant, but that was the role Andrew spent most of his time filling nonetheless. It was administrative work, helping with personnel issues. He was given a small office, a phone and a computer and was bored out of his tree most of the time. I must admit, the idea of Andrew trapped behind a desk is still one I have a hard time wrapping my head around.

In September he started taking part-time graduate studies in counter-insurgency. RMC was offering a course in Petawawa, with additional courses in Ottawa at National Defence Headquarters, in order to make it readily available for personnel. Classes were once a week, and Andrew would drive two hours each way to attend. His position at RHQ certainly didn't demand much of him, and though it was a long drive to attend the three-hour class, it was better than the busywork they had him doing. Andrew wanted to believe that he'd be able to pursue some kind of career within Canadian Forces though he was beginning to suspect that it might not be in Artillery.

On November 18, 2002, we filed a new amended PRB grievance detailing our concerns with Col Ward's response, and once again we requested that it be forwarded to CDS as Final Authority. It would be a very long time before we heard anything from the office of the Chief of the Defence Staff.

Andrew came home on his Christmas leave. It was always good to see him, even if only briefly. Especially since the McBride household counted on his attending to our computer needs on these annual visits, which he viewed as including upgrading of our computers and operating system.

On February 6 of 2003, we received notice of a pending Administrative Review to consider release—no actual date was mentioned, only that it was pending. It is worth pointing out that this was *eleven months* after the word had been passed to his regiment that he *was* being released. Needless to say, the de facto release by degrees which Andrew had been subjected to didn't leave us with a great deal of confidence that the pending Administrative Review was going to be much more than a formality.

On March 4, we filed an objection to release based on the rather conspicuous fact that, nineteen months on, the hearing which had actually *initiated* the release proceedings was still under appeal. This objection, as far as I can tell, had no effect whatsoever, but it needed to be filed so that it would be part of the record.

Canadian Forces' *modus operandi* was, by this point, pretty clear. A recommendation for release springs from a flawed PRB hearing that raises a legitimate grievance. Rather than address the grievance responsibly, simply delay and pretend that the issues brought up aren't legitimate. An Administrative Review will eventually be scheduled, regardless of the grievance process.

In late July, Andrew received word that an Administrative Review had taken place in Ottawa on June 23. Brigadier-General Paul Hussey, Director General Military Careers, had decided that Andrew was to be released upon completion of his compulsory service, which was to say five years after his graduation on May 2, 2004.

The decision message had come to LCol Cotten, and Andrew was given a copy. He noticed right away that it included a factual error: it stated that he had been placed on C&P (Counselling and Probation). We wrote to the DGCM on July 11, pointing out Andrew had never been placed on C&P. In the same letter we asked for a copy of the *actual* decision itself.

From July of 2003 to January of 2004, LCol Cotten, along with 190 members of 2RCHA, were deployed to Afghanistan on Operation ATHENA. Had circumstances played out even slightly differently back in July of 2001, Andrew might have been deployed there as well. As it was, he was cooling his heels behind a desk in regimental HQ. With LCol Cotten overseas, the command of remaining 2RCHA personnel fell to Major Bart Gauvin, Cotten's second in command.

An amended decision message came through Maj Gauvin on July 22. The actual decision was again not provided.

We filed a short grievance to the Hussey decision, on September 12, which referenced all the previous documents. The gist of that grievance was obvious; Hussey's decision (as best as we could tell without a copy of the document itself) was predicated on an earlier decision which was itself fundamentally flawed and being reviewed by the Chief of the Defence Staff.

Less than a week later, however, Maj Gauvin wrote that we were to refile a comprehensive grievance integrating all previous grievances into one document—but that was not all.

In that same letter, he also refused to provide a copy of the decision, suggesting that we had received a copy back in February. This was peculiar seeing as the Administrate Review itself was ostensibly only held on June 23. Then again, *perhaps* he was accidentally parroting a message sent back to *him* from BGen Hussey. It is possible that the decision had already been made when Andrew received his notice of the 'upcoming' review, and if so, perhaps a copy of the decision *had* been sent LCol Cotten back in February. For that matter, it was possible that the decision had been made long before even that. Remember, word that Andrew was being released had trickled down as far as Captain Hunter as early as March 2002. In short, it was entirely possible that the entire release 'process' was all just for show.

We set to work on a comprehensive grievance to the Hussey decision. It took us over two months to prepare and included three three-ring binders worth of documents. It was filed with Maj Gauvin on November 28, 2003.

I remember feeling at loose ends in December. On the one hand I was relieved that the ball was once again in CF's court. On the other hand I was getting less hopeful that the play they were going to make with the ball was going to be genuine and honest. While there was a grievance process in place, no one in CF seemed to be taking it seriously. They were simply going through the motions while they moved ahead with their own agenda. Andrew's release date was in six months and, unless someone in CF decided to own up to the facts and actually take responsibility, those six months would drain away before we knew it.

I was exhausted. Andrew was discouraged, and I suspected he was starting to fray around the edges. Kerry too was frustrated at a process that had claimed so much of my time over the past couple of years, especially since I couldn't promise her a resolution any time soon. In some ways, I think it was worse for Kerry because she wasn't participating. She was stuck on the sidelines in an ongoing debacle that threatened the livelihood of her eldest son, robbed her of endless evenings and weekends with me, and brought a great deal of gloom and anger into the household.

It was in December that I picked up the *Lamer Report*. It had come out in November, but I was up to my neck in Andrew's case when it first came to my attention. The Right Honourable Antonio Lamer had been the 16th Chief Justice of Canada, having served in that capacity from July of 1990 to January 2000. A highly-respected jurist, it fell to him to write the first independent review of Bill C-25, *An Act to amend the National Defence Act and to make consequential amendments to other Acts.* The bill, which had received royal assent in December of 1998, contained a clause requiring that the Minister of National Defence undertake to have an independent review of amendments to the National Defence Act every five years.

Apart from being a former Chief Justice, Antonio Lamer had also served in the Royal Canadian Artillery and the Canadian Intelligence Corps as a young man, making him uniquely suited to the task. He began the review in March 2003, and it was tabled in the House of Commons on November 5, 2003, by Minister of National Defence John McCallum.

While Former Chief Justice Lamer felt that many of the amendments were working well, he had some serious reservations about the Canadian Forces grievance process. When I read the report, I must admit, it felt like a much-needed wind was gathering and that perhaps it would fill our sails.

> "Soldiers are not second-class citizens. They are entitled to be treated with respect, and in the case of the grievance process, in a procedurally fair manner. This

is a fundamental principle that must not be lost in a bureaucratic process, even a military one."

—Former Chief Justice Antonio Lamer

Nine

March 2004. It had been over two and a half years since the incident with Capt Bobbitt, and nothing had been resolved. Two years since the news of his de facto release had been sent to his regiment. More than a year and a half since he'd been pulled from the guns. Sixteen months without so much as a peep from the Chief of the Defence Staff on the PRB grievance. Nine months since the ostensive Hussey decision to release and four months with no word on the grievance of *that* decision. Andrew was scheduled to be released in less than two months' time.

Andrew was demoralized. His once-bright hopes of a military career lay tarnished at his feet. His relationship with the regiment had crumbled because, from their perspective, he was now little more than a liability. They were limited in how they could use him, but he was still on their books and they could not request a new junior officer to take his place. To be fair, it really *was* a ridiculous untenable situation—but that was hardly Andrew's fault.

In contrast to the willful negligence CF showed the grievance process, when it came to the release process they were remarkably efficient. In the run up to Andrew's release they had already started to expedite things. For instance, he had already been told he was being evicted from the Russia House, his home for the past four years. While upsetting, it only made sense—everyone including Andrew could see that, for even if some last-minute miracle turned the tide on his grievances and he was saved from release, he certainly could not serve in 2RCHA at this point.

The one bright spot in Andrew's life at that point was a young woman he'd started dating back in November. Her name was Jemma, and a mutual friend had introduced them. A lovely girl, she lived in the town of Arnprior just west of Ottawa and was going to teachers college.

On Monday March 22, Andrew walked into the regimental headquarters to find that his computer and phone had been taken away. He stood in the doorway to his empty office for a minute and had to accept that he was out of a job. He considered talking to either Maj Gauvin or LCol Cotten but knew that there was no point in doing so. What could be said that hadn't been said already? He was a dead man walking, and he knew it.

As he left the building, it all hit him harder than he would have expected. Not wishing to return to the Russia House, he found himself walking into the next building and seeking out the office of Capt Sandi Scott, the regimental padre. Captain Scott was there, and he could tell Andrew was upset. They spoke for a while before Sandi asked if he could take Andrew to see someone at the health centre. Andrew was clearly upset, and perhaps they could, at the very least, prescribe something to help him relax. Andrew agreed.

The nurse who interviewed him was concerned. Andrew's story was upsetting him, and she could understand why. This second lieutenant had been under mounting stress for some time, and now things were coming to a head as his release date approached. When she had finished with her assessment, she excused herself and brought in the medical officer. The 2RCHA medical officer had changed since 2002, and it was now Captain Ethan Davenport.

Dr. Davenport sat and talked with Andrew for some time, and he managed to convince Andrew that he should go to Ottawa for a full assessment. Andrew was exhausted by this point and didn't bother arguing.

I learned later that Dr. Davenport had requested an ambulance to take Andrew to Ottawa. An ambulance wasn't available, however; which is why Andrew was transported instead in a Military Police van. And because he was being transported in a Military Police van, protocol dictated that he be seated between two MPs.

And that he be shackled.

I guess the MPs were sorry to have to shackle him, but Andrew just shrugged it off. He was beyond caring at that point. At least the officers were sorry; that was more than could be said for any of the men trying to railroad him.

When Andrew was escorted into the psychiatric ward of the Civic Hospital in shackles, most of the other folks were somewhat unnerved—all but one guy, sitting alone on one of the seats. When he saw Andrew he grinned and sat up straight.

"Now *that's* my kinda guy!"

It was Sandi Scott who called me to let me know that Andrew had been taken to Ottawa.

I flew down on March 24, 2004, and attended the release meeting with the hospital psychiatrists. The plan was to remove Andrew from the source of his stress and effect a program to work through it. It's not as though he had a job waiting for him on the base. Andrew was released from the hospital and planned to stay with a friend in Ottawa which would facilitate being an outpatient to the hospital. I would be staying with the same friend that night and before heading back to Nanaimo.

Because Andrew's car was still at Russia House, Jemma offered to drive him there to pick it up. It seemed like a good plan, and so I settled in at the friend's apartment. Andrew and I could talk about where things were headed with the grievance and the deadlines when he got back.

Two hours later I got a call from Jemma. She was near hysterical, for as soon as they had arrived at the base, Andrew had been arrested. Military Police had been watching Russia House and when

Andrew showed up he was confronted, cuffed and arrested. I'm not exactly sure how it played out but there were a number of MPs and the scene had left Jemma badly shaken. When I asked her what he'd been arrested *for*, she said didn't know and that it happened quite fast.

When I got off the phone with her, I called the Brigade Duty Officer and asked him to go to Russia House to calm her down and help ensure she got home okay. I don't remember the young man's name, but he was very cooperative and I really appreciated that. Of course, I had no way of getting to Petawawa at that point and had to wait until the next day to catch a bus to the base.

I boarded a Greyhound at the Catherine Street station the next morning at around ten. It would take me right into CFB Petawawa though, with stops along the way, it would take around three hours. I was concerned for Andrew and more than a little annoyed at this latest flash of CF nonsense.

When I spoke to Capt Davenport, he apologized for having ordered the arrest. When he called the Civic Hospital and found out Andrew had been released, he didn't know where he'd gone. Having lost track of him, Davenport put out an arrest warrant in order to detain Andrew if he showed back up at the base. I was skeptical. When he talked to the folks at the Civic Hospital, what he would have found out was that Andrew was deemed not a threat, which is why he was released in the first place.

I attended the release meeting with the Custody Review Officer, and Andrew was released from detention. No charges would be pressed.

It was clear Andrew was angry and depressed. He felt betrayed by the way CF was treating him. He was mentally exhausted from handling his appeals for the past three years and from working in a difficult work environment for the past two. A decision was made to post Andrew to the Area Support Unit of Canadian Forces Base Kingston pending his release. And in the meantime he would bunk with his friend in Ottawa while seeing someone at the Civic on an outpatient basis.

We decided to apply to the Federal Court for a stay of release pending the Initial Authority response on the Hussey decision because it was clear that the powers that be at CF were simply running out the clock. Not being a trial lawyer, I enlisted the help of my old partner, Peter Ramsay. Ramsay Lampman Rhodes is a well-established and respected firm out of Nanaimo, and Peter is an accomplished trial lawyer who had been named Queen's Counsel in 1999. The hope was that, by staying the release, it would light a fire under the appropriate asses to move the process forward.

Understand that when you are engaged in a legal battle with the Canadian Forces—or any government agency or department—the government is represented by lawyers from the Department of Justice. You have to pay for your own representation while the government simply taps the DOJ. You are in effect paying to go up against your own tax dollars. Needless to say, your financial resources never stack up very well against your opponent's under those circumstances. For this reason you need to know what you're doing, because the playing field is not level.

We filed an application for a stay on March 26, 2004.

As predicted, this move got folks' attention. It resulted in an agreement between Ramsay and CF counsel, a Department of Justice lawyer by the name of Ken Manning, that the release date would be moved to July 2 to enable a response on the release grievance. That was contingent, however, on Peter filing a notice of discontinuance—i.e., that we withdraw our request for a stay. Peter filed the discontinuance. It seemed that CF did not want *anyone* outside of CF holding them to account. It was also clear that part of their strategy had involved deliberate delay on the grievances while proceeding with release so as to complete the latter before the former could be brought to bear.

In April of 2004, LCol Ken Haeck, the officer under whose careful scrutiny this entire fiasco was born, retired from regular forces. As we will soon see, there were plenty of officers of a similar calibre willing to soldier on without him.

In June the Initial Authority response to the Hussey grievance came down. It had been considered by none other than MGen (having been promoted) Hussey himself, making him the second high-ranking officer to disregard official protocol and review his own ruling. To pretend for even an instant that the Director General of Military Careers (a Major-General no less) was unaware of the basic protocols for the assignment of an IA is simply not credible. This was a disregarding of the rules governing the process and illustrates a systemic willingness to flaunt protocols when it suited the CF's ends.

MGen Hussey did not hold a hearing, reviewing only the written record, hence there was no new evidence on the issue of the order having been passed to Andrew. No surprise, he upheld his own prior decision, refusing redress in a response dated June 21, 2004.

Hussey had based his initial 2003 decision entirely on the finding of the 2001 Progress Review Board. However, in his IA response to the grievance, he insisted that he was *precluded* from looking at the PRB decision as it was under appeal, which is peculiar insofar as said grievance process predated his 2003 decision by more than a year and a half. At no point did he acknowledge this or admit that there existed any inconsistency in his current stance.

It would be easy to dismiss this as simply idiocy, but it wasn't. This was, as I said, a deliberate gaming of the process to burn through time and move ahead with an agenda they weren't willing to negotiate.

That same day, we had Peter Ramsay file a second application for an interim order staying Andrew's release pending finalization of his two outstanding grievances. Predictably, CF strongly opposed the motion.

Eight days later, on June 29, Mr. Justice Kelen ordered CF to refrain from releasing Andrew pending the final decision with respect to his outstanding grievances. In his reasons for judgment, the Justice noted that "The CF grievance process has not been working in a timely fashion for the Applicant" and that he "needed to have his grievances adjudicated without unreasonable delay, i.e., in a matter of months."

Ken Manning, counsel for CF had, in the *Memorandum of Fact and Law of the Respondent,* claimed that a restraining order would have the effect of undermining confidence in CF's ability to carry out its mandate.

It's important to recognize that no one was saying they could not release Andrew, only that they needed to process the outstanding grievances *first.* The fact that it required a court order to enforce such basic common sense is staggering. The problem, of course, was that it was growing increasingly clear by that point that releasing Andrew *fairly* was simply not going to be feasible.

Mr. Manning made no mention on CF's behalf of the fact that Andrew's case *could* have been resolved at any time in the previous three years by simply affording Andrew basic procedural fairness.

Subsequently, we wrote numerous letters to CF and to the Canadian Forces Grievance Board urging action on moving the two grievances forward.

On July 9, 2004, an amended release grievance was filed and sent to Chief of the Defence Staff for Final Authority. That same month, Colonel Michael Ward, former head of the Combat Training Centre, was promoted to Brigadier-General and assumed command of the Canadian Army's Land Force Doctrine and Training System. And Major-General Paul Hussey, former Director General of Military Careers, took command of the Canadian Defence Academy in Kingston.

What many people perhaps fail to appreciate is just how fluid these positions are. Officers drift into and out of postings that often have little if anything to do with each other, and they do so every two or three years. For a successful officer on the rise, the positions represent more and more responsibility but never with much time to learn the new roles before they are posted elsewhere. The culture of advancement, while it benefits the individuals, does very little to ensure much practical experience in the specifics of the roles themselves. Even the position of Chief of the Defence Staff (the senior military commander within CF) is a role only ever held briefly—the last posting in a successful career before retirement. From 1996 to 2014, that position has been held by no less than seven different individuals, for an average of less than three years per posting.

July was also when Andrew's posting to ASU Kingston finally went through. Andrew had been bunking with another friend in Newmarket—after his friend from Ottawa had been reassigned—and seeing a CF psychiatrist by the name of Dr. David Ewing who operated out of the Canadian Forces Health Services Centre at CFB Borden. When his posting to Kingston went through, it meant that he'd have to commute to Borden on a regular basis to keep seeing Dr. Ewing. On the plus side, it also meant he'd be able to move into military quarters in Kingston in the fall and take full-time courses in counter-insurgency (COIN) at RMC. Even after all that had happened, he was trying to look forward and position himself for a new role within the Canadian Forces. Andrew still wanted to serve and chose to look upon his experience as being symptomatic of a broken part of a larger worthwhile whole.

Another funny story, this one from his first term of full-time COIN studies at RMC: Andrew was walking across campus when a large black sedan drove by bearing the flag of a Two Leaf General. He stopped walking and gave the car a brief salute as protocol suggested. When he turned to continue walking he noticed that the vehicle pulled to a halt up ahead. As Andrew approached, the sergeant rolled down his window:

"Major-General Hussey has asked me to tell you that you are the only individual to salute his car today and he thanks you for that."

The sergeant then rolled his window back up and the car drove off. Andrew could only shake his head and continue to class.

On February 4, 2005, General Rick Hillier was appointed Chief of the Defence Staff by then Prime Minister Paul Martin, replacing Gen Raymond Henault. Though it had been more than two years since we had filed Andrew's PRB grievance it never saw Henault's desk. It was still with the grievance board. The CFGB was backlogged and a severe bottleneck in the system. And even once a decision was passed from the CFGB to the Chief of the Defence staff there was nothing compelling the CDS to respond in a timely manner. In fact, there was nothing officially compelling him to respond at all.

In the normal course of events, none of this is an issue from CF's perspective—in fact, it comes in handy—because they are happy to release members while grievances are outstanding. However, in Andrew's case, our court order meant that he *couldn't* be released without a response, which put us at a stalemate with CF.

Time marched on, and that summer Andrew started writing a counter-insurgency training manual as a self-directed project. It seemed like a natural extension of the courses he was taking and a decent project to help him distill what he was learning. The Preface would in time set out its rationale and objective, as well as 'lessons learned:'

> In 9/11 I was a soldier in conventional forces trained to conduct conventional warfare in a conventional war. Preparing to counter guerrillas and terrorists in an irregular war required a significant adjustment in learning. The challenge lay not in a lack of information about countering insurgency but in its overabundance: how to distill useful information and put it into useable

form. This vehicle is an outcome of tackling that challenge. [...]

Two important lessons about countering insurgency were gleaned from my research. The first lesson is that learning while countering insurgency is not an academic exercise—it is essential. Insurgents attack, the state responds, the insurgents adapt, the state adjusts its response and so on, *ad infinitum*. Learning, and applying that learning, is synonymous with countering insurgency. The second lesson is that success in countering insurgency requires all factors in war be addressed. Just some, or perhaps even most of them, is not good enough. Countering insurgency is like an orchestra performing: all factors have to be worked together. All factors addressed poorly is better than only some well. Failure to apply these two lessons means, at best, a higher expenditure of lives and national treasure than necessary, or at worst, defeat.

He brought early drafts of it to my friend Charlie Whisker who was only too eager to tear into it and make suggestions. It was good to see Andrew throw himself into it, and I really felt that perhaps counter-insurgency was what he would step into if we were ever to get his grievances cleared up. Nothing seemed to be moving on that front, however.

In October of 2005, the consolidated PRB and PRB release appeals were still outstanding. Gen Hillier had not ruled even though the grievance board had finally, after more than two and a half years of delay, forwarded their recommendations to him in June. The problem was that the CFGB confirmed what we had been saying all along: there had been fatal defects with the PRB and release decisions and their appeals. The court order put them in a tough position. They could not release Andrew without addressing his grievances and the CFGB findings were pretty unequivocal.

And so, knowing they would need to move forward (and what the decision would have to be) they first set in motion a new avenue for release: Medical Employment Limitations (MELs) something they felt the court was less likely to block them on. In essence they were going to go after Andrew for his mental breakdown and paint him as no longer deployable. This despite the fact that his so-called mental breakdown was a direct result of the stress that they themselves had subjected him to.

Of course, true to form, they didn't bother with procedural fairness in their pursuit of the MELs release because, by this point in Andrew's case, the ends were held to be more important than the means. They had bungled things from the start and failed to do the right thing time and time again, and now the situation was festering as a result. They even had the federal court watching them. They had ruined a potentially promising officer and felt that Andrew was now never going to be someone they could have in the officer corps. It was a bad situation, and they needed it to be over.

You might well ask: *Why, then, did they not handle the MELs release in a procedurally impeccable manner, considering the route that had led them to this place?* It is a good question. Arrogance, maybe, or simply anger at being challenged. Or perhaps they felt that ultimately a MELs decision was something that even the courts would not be willing to challenge.

Major Linda Garand MD, from the office of the Director of Medical Policy, assigned "permanent MELs" to Andrew by a Medical Statement dated October 20, 2005.

Andrew had received no prior notification of the assignment of MELs. Only after the MELs were assigned was he provided with the notification in a copy of a communication from NDHQ to ASU/ CFB Kingston dated October 31, 2005. There had been neither disclosure nor an opportunity for input at this step in the process.

On January 2, we filed a MELs grievance, and the next day made what would be our first request of many for disclosure regarding the decision.

On January 12, 2006, four and a half *years* after being falsely accused of lying, the Chief of the Defence Staff, General Hillier, granted redress on both outstanding grievances. While he decided to accept as fact that Andrew had been passed the order to move, he ruled (as he more or less had to) that Andrew had seen very little in the way of procedural fairness and that the conclusions of the hearing needed to be disregarded. As a result, Andrew was granted Phase IV training and promoted to Lieutenant (retroactive May 2000) and Captain (retroactive May 2002).

Even four and a half years after the fact, the Chief of the Defence Staff took it upon himself to decide that Andrew had been passed the order to move, notwithstanding that he (like Haeck, Ward, and Hussey before him) did not have sufficient proof to make such a decision. Of course, it could be argued that he was in effect deciding not to disagree with Haeck, Ward and Hussey. Still, the important thing was that, unlike Haeck, Ward and Hussey, he actually responded to the substance of our grievances.

When he learned of the grant of redress, on January 31, Andrew left an excited phone message for us. I emailed him, sharing in the great news. His email back referred to his making an application to the recently-activated CSOR (Canadian Special Operations Regiment). While CF's handling of the PRB and its appeals had screwed around with his life for almost five years, he remained hopeful that he could still have a career in CF. It is why he had continued with war studies and remained physically fit to Army standards while waiting on a resolution.

In his MELs grievance, just ten days before, he had stated, "There is nothing wrong with me medically that would probably not be put right upon CF putting right my PRB of July 31, 2001."

For that reason he was confident that he'd be able to put his health issues behind him, be reassessed and get his career back on track.

Part 3:
Friendly Fire

Ten

Friendly fire is, of course, being used ironically here. Typically it is a term used to describe situations leading to the unintended casualties of a fellow soldier—but there was nothing unintentional about what CF was doing. Andrew, by this point, was not collateral damage; he was an intended target.

And again, perhaps some pre-emptive clarification is in order. No one is suggesting that the CF should be unable to judge for itself if an individual is fit for duty. No one is even suggesting that Andrew himself should have been given some sort of free pass based on the outrageous treatment that actually led to his mental breakdown. What I *am* saying is that the MELs process was invoked and used disingenuously as a convenient workaround when it became clear that CF was going to be held to account and forced to back down from their initial attempt to release Andrew.

After running roughshod over procedural fairness for four and a half years—trying to force a result in order to rid themselves of what they perceived as a problem—they decided to stay the course and force a result ostensibly using the MELs process.

My problem was never with the MELs process *per se.* My problem was with CF's deliberate and selective *circumvention* of the process in order to force the issue. Had CF decided to play the MELs process by the book, in a way that was serious and straightforward, there would simply have been no basis for a grievance. The problem is that, had they done so, they might not have credibly gotten the result they hoped for, and so, rather than risk it, they superficially used MELs as no more than a cover, a means to an end.

To recap, on October 31, 2005, Andrew was notified, after the fact, that he had been assigned so-called "permanent MELs" on October 20 by Major Garand MD from the D Med Pol office. There had been no disclosure of any kind and no opportunity for input. Presumably this was in reference to Andrew's breakdown of March 22, 2004, but of course there was no way to know for sure, and seeing as *that* had been nineteen months previous and considering the state of play of his ongoing struggle with CF, it smacked of tactics.

Now, were circumstances different, one might afford CF the benefit of the doubt in terms of their motives, but there had been precious little in the previous four and a half years to suggest that that was warranted.

Without trying to downplay Andrew's breakdown, it is worth pointing out that it *was* as a direct result of very specific protracted stressors which had come together (either by chance or design) in March of 2004. These stressors were the product of Andrew's ongoing mistreatment at the hands of CF. Also worth reiterating the scope and nature of the breakdown: Andrew *voluntarily* went in to speak with the padre who called a nurse who alerted the medical officer who (as it turned out) had Andrew taken to Ottawa in shackles by the Military Police and was later responsible for having him arrested when he came back for his car. How much of that was warranted? Who knows? How much of that played out the way it did for other reasons? Again, who knows? But to pretend that there exists no room for speculation would be naïve.

On January 3, 2006, in our first of many letters requesting proper disclosure, I wrote:

> I have nothing in this new attempt at release other than Refs. A and B [Notice of Decision dated October

20, 2005, and Case Management Action Plan dated December 5, 2005] and accordingly I request full particulars as to what CF is doing here. That should include copies of any and all documents relating to this administrative process, including the evidence on which this decision was made.

The Director of Medical Policy was forwarded both the grievance and the disclosure request on January 5 and acknowledged receipt of same on January 9—though this and so much more would only be disclosed to us years later. Whether acting on his own volition or under orders from on high, he did not respond.

When, on January 12, 2006, the Hillier decision came down and Andrew was afforded redress for four and half years of mistreatment by CF, we were both very pleased, and Andrew was, for the first time in years, genuinely hopeful. He had been promoted to captain, and now that all the stressors that had led to his breakdown in 2004 had been addressed, it was just a matter of putting the MELs to bed and moving forward with his career.

Andrew's hope was misplaced, however, for the sad truth was that CF never had any intention of letting Andrew move forward; though they had conceded defeat in their previous attempt to release him, they did so only after they had put in place a new endgame.

In a letter to the CDS dated February 21, 2006, Andrew accepted the grant of redress, noting that while there were erroneous findings of fact in the decision, he was focused on a return to active duty. Buoyed by what now seemed like a turning of the tide, Andrew decided to submit the current draft of his training manual to a US military contest; it was really more of an essay contest looking for papers on counterinsurgency, but Andrew thought that there was no harm in submitting the manual that he and Charlie had worked on together. Andrew's newfound optimism, however, wasn't to last for long.

On March 8, 2006, Andrew was given notice of an upcoming AR/MEL. No date was given for the Administrative Review, and we were given fifteen days to prepare a submission. Along with the notice, CF provided us with a so-called disclosure package that contained copies of a notification of change of employment limitations (Form CF-2088), a Medical Statement dated October 20, 2005, an Accommodation Statement dated February 3, 2006, and a Synopsis (Recommendation) dated February 17, 2006.

What the disclosure package conspicuously did *not* contain was any relevant information necessary to meet and challenge the MELs and thus the recommendation that he be released. It contained no real medical diagnosis or prognosis, nor did it provide the information necessary for an *independent* medical professional to know exactly what needed to be proved or disproved during the AR/MEL process. None of the documents contained information on the medical standards or other guidelines followed by Garand to arrive at a decision to assign permanent MELs and release on medical grounds.

I again wrote to CF on March 13, 2006, raising its failure to disclose the relevant evidence and information:

> The CF has not disclosed the case McBride must meet and consequently he is unable to properly prepare his representations to you. The CF has merely provided administrative records showing that on certain dates certain officers made certain decisions; it has not provided the evidence on which those decisions were based nor the reasoning behind them. Ref. C [my letter of January 3] was a request for full disclosure.

These requests for disclosure were not trivial. Because Garand's decision to impose MELs had been without notice or disclosure of *any* kind, it meant that the AR/MEL process was to be the only opportunity for Andrew to obtain and consider the evidence and the reasoning behind the decision to assign MELs and recommend his release from CF. We needed to assess the veracity of that evidence: was it direct or hearsay; was it in context or taken out of context; was it true or false. Having determined its veracity, medical professionals would have needed to see the relevant information to evaluate Garand's and CF Medical Officers' assessments, diagnosis and prognosis, and to make their own diagnosis and prognosis. To do so, Andrew's doctors would also have needed to know the guidelines and policies that had influenced and shaped opinions and decisions of Garand and the other CF medical officers.

In my letter of March 13, 2006, requesting disclosure, I went on to state:

> Based on our experience in these matters, we assume CF will not provide full disclosure and accordingly we have begun preparing Capt McBride's representations.

Without the necessary information, I provided representations, dated March 16, 2006, as best as I could. As was par for the course, it would be a very long time before we heard anything on that score.

In June, however, Andrew *did* hear from an unexpected military source—this one from *outside* of CF. Though the counter-insurgency contest he'd entered had closed (with a winner presumably announced) Andrew received a letter from Lieutenant General David Petraeus who had been the first commander of the Multi-National Security Transition Command in Iraq (MNSTC-I) from June 2004 to September 2005. Andrew's manual had made it to the lieutenant general's desk, and Petraeus, who would later assume the Directorship of the CIA, took the time to write a letter of commendation urging Andrew to keep up the good work. While this letter certainly gave Andrew a small thrill, it was bittersweet because Charlie Whisker, who had given enthusiastic feedback and suggestions on early drafts, was very sick, having been diagnosed with prostate cancer the previous year.

Charlie Whisker passed away on August 11, and his death hit us all very hard. He was only sixty-eight years old when he finally succumbed to the cancer. Far too young. Charlie had never lost interest in Andrew's career, and I remember how pleased he had been in January when he'd heard about the Hillier decision and Andrew's promotion. With Charlie's health in decline, we never talked much about the subsequent MELs situation, and of that I am glad.

Ten days after Charlie's death and still mourning his loss, I requested that the MELs appeal be forwarded to a Final Authority which is the griever's right when CF does not handle a grievance within the timeline permitted.

Eleven

"Dad, something's happened." It was October and Andrew's voice on the phone sounded tense. "They are definitely processing me for release."

"They must have held the review and made a decision."

"But we didn't hear anything. Can they *do* that?"

At this point nothing surprised me.

"I want you to start asking questions on your end. When I get off the phone with you, I'll start making calls and shaking some trees."

—

The first person I called was Peter Ramsay. He didn't like the sound of what was going on and went right to work on a Federal Court application for a stay pending FA on the MELs release decision. That was the right call as it turns out. Neither Andrew nor I got anywhere, but as soon as the application was filed on November 1, CF and the DOJ came out of the woodwork. CF counsel this time was one Lisa Riddle. It turned out that Andrew's pending release date was November 17, 2006. Ramsay promptly requested a copy of the release decision.

On December 1, 2006, CF actually deigned to disclose the results of the decision, and we received a copy of the AR/MEL decision to proceed with release by LCol Taillefer, the Director Military

Careers and Resource Management. That decision was dated April 18, 2006.

On December 5, Ramsay again settled with CF. Andrew's release date would be moved to June 23, 2007, again contingent upon Ramsay filing a discontinuance. He did so.

CF had also issued a decision message dated May 6, 2006, and a release instruction message dated May 8, 2006. We received copies of these messages during a December 13 meeting. Andrew's attendance had been requested for that meeting, and Major E.A. Schofield, as CF representative, took the opportunity to give Andrew formal notice of his upcoming release.

What we didn't receive at that meeting was any explanation whatsoever as to *why* these documents were not sent to us automatically—why we received them eight months after the fact and only *then* after we requested them.

Perhaps a credible explanation can be found in Paragraph 3.D of the decision message of May 6:

> Should member's medical fitness improve to the degree that the member is able to perform the generic tasks required to meet the U of S requirement, a new AR/MEL will be held. Should this occur, new statements must be submitted to D Med Pol through normal medical channels for approval before release.

CF had specifically ordered the MELs ruling, whose evidence and guidelines they subsequently refused to disclose, *prior* to announcing the Hillier FA response and redress, knowing full well that the issues leading to Andrew's breakdown were directly related to the unresolved nature of the grievances. Then they pushed through an AR/MEL to look at that ruling without having initiated anything in the way of a follow-up assessment, even though they knew that the resolution of the grievance would address the precipitating factors of the MELs ruling.

They had then deliberately burned through almost eight months without disclosing the decision so as to limit our ability to respond in a timely manner. There was no longer even a pretence about what was happening. CF was simply going to force the matter through by all means necessary without so much as a nod to procedural fairness.

On January 26, 2007, we filed a MELs release grievance, and it was consolidated with the January 2, 2006 MELs grievance and both were sent to General Hillier, the Chief of the Defence Staff as FA. We had been fighting this thing for five and a half years. Andrew had just turned twenty-four when his relationship with Capt Bobbitt had sparked a bogus progress review board hearing on the last day of the final exercise at CTC Gagetown. If we were unable to turn the tide, he would be thirty when CF finally managed to muscle him out. The time, energy, and resources that had disappeared into this struggle by that point was hard to wrap my head around, and all because CF refused to address issues honestly and responsibly.

While we were finishing up this final grievance submission, Dan Bobbitt (now a Major) was preparing to deploy to Kandahar. He was to command D Battery as part of the 2nd Battalion Royal Canadian Regiment Battle Group.

Twelve

On June 13, 2007, Peter Ramsay received a letter stating that Andrew had been released from CF effective June 12. This date was carefully chosen for two reasons. First, it was six months to the day since Andrew had received his formal notice of release. Second— and this really was a stroke of Machiavellian genius—it was ten days *before* the negotiated release date agreed upon when we filed the second discontinuance and before we had a chance to file for another stay.

CF had straight-up broken their word. They had lied. It cannot be spun any other way. The fact that this whole SNAFU was sparked in July of 2001 by one zealous captain's unfounded assertion of a lie on Andrew's part was, I am sure, lost on them by this point. Though some *might* argue that the PRB fiasco *had* been redressed by Gen Hillier and that this was a separate matter, I would disagree. The MELs process was nothing more than cover used to finish what was started by other means.

And this was the beginning of the end game.

By claiming Andrew's release was a *fait accompli*, they were deliberately attempting to change the complexion of things. Whereas before we had been asking that CF wait until they had addressed the outstanding grievances, now it would be framed as us petitioning for his reinstatement.

What was most shocking to me about this was that Lisa Riddle did not excuse herself from the case over that stunt; in my experience, she certainly should have. Agreements between counsel need to be honoured—otherwise, the ability for counsel to negotiate agreements at all is directly compromised.

On June 19, 2007, we again applied to the Federal Court for a stay regarding the MELs release. As we had with our last stay, the one we'd been tricked into discontinuing, we pointed out that the MELs ruling upon which the release was predicated was problematic and was the subject of an ongoing grievance. We also pointed out that CF had flagrantly contravened a previously-negotiated agreement by moving to release prior to June 23. Furthermore, by failing to obtain the consent of the Governor General—something that must be done whenever an officer is released—their so-called release of June 12 was not valid.

On August 29, 2007, CF decided to go back and tie up a conspicuous loose end; they approached the office of Governor General Michaëlle Jean and sought Her Excellency's approval. They obtained it on August 31 and then claimed that this approval was effective to June 12, 2007. Of course, they had no legal basis for claiming backdated approval, but considering the scope and scale of other liberties they had already taken they didn't care. So long as no one challenged them on it and it didn't come back to bite them, they had no qualms about that little manoeuvre.

Court Registry scheduled the hearing on our application for a stay for December 13, 2007 and on December 14, Justice Barnes refused to grant an order restraining CF from releasing pending completion of outstanding grievances. Considering that we had previously been granted a stay by Justice Kelen under similar circumstances, this came as a disappointment. Of course, one thing was noticeably different this time around.

Riddle had, in the *Memorandum of Fact and Law of the Respondent*, claimed:

> CF must be allowed to release members who are unfit
> for service. This is of benefit to other members that

might be injured by being required to work along-side members who are not fit for service. It must be emphasized that what the Applicant is seeking to do is demand that he be allowed to serve in CF despite the fact he is not medically fit for service. A restraining order of this nature significantly harms the ability of CF to ensure the safety of its members.

And, ultimately, this was the stance that CF *knew* would back the courts off. That it was, in Andrew's case, a ridiculous disingenuous characterization was neither here nor there. CF counsel trotted it out without shame. They knew that, when the stay was framed against the supposed safety of other members of CF, the judge would back down. I suspect Barnes was not the first to be backed off with this.

The MELs process was simply another weapon in the CF arsenal. It is a powerful weapon intended to address serious specific issues, but CF certainly wasn't above using it for their own purposes when things had not gone their way.

The timing of the decision made things difficult. When a federal court judge renders an interim decision, you have only ten days to file an appeal. It was mid-December, and with the decision coming when it did, Peter Ramsay was simply not available. I counted myself lucky to be able to retain the services of Douglas Schmitt at Alexander Holburn Beaudin and Lang. It was a complicated case, and Douglas was coming into it cold, but he managed to file our appeal with an hour to spare on Christmas Eve 2007.

While Barnes was a real blow, and the chance of winning an appeal on an interim motion were slim, I felt we had some valid concerns and that the Barnes decision was weak. Also, and I can admit this now, Riddle's Memo of Fact and Law was simply too galling to let slide.

With the appeal filed, the case was again out of our hands.

On July 1, 2008, General Rick Hillier retired from the Canadian Forces without having rendered a FA decision on the MELs grievances. The problem, again, was that almost two years after they had been filed, they were still gathering dust at the CFGB. The eventual findings (still more than a year and a half away, I might add) would fall to Hillier's replacement, General Walter Natynczyk.

Thirteen

On September 16, 2008, our appeal was heard by Justices of Appeal Robert Décary, Pierre Blais and Michael Ryer and the decision was delivered from the bench. The decision is quite brief, and so it is reproduced below in its entirety.

[1] Mr. McBride was released from the Canadian Forces on June 12, 2007.

[2] On June 19, 2007, Mr. McBride sought an interim injunction restraining the Canadian Forces from releasing him pending the resolution of what he refers to as his Grievance Procedure.

[3] On December 14, 2007, Barnes J. denied the interim injunction.

[4] On December 24, 2007, the appellant initiated an appeal to this Court in which he seeks an order restraining the Canadian Forces from releasing him prior to the expiry of his term of service, i.e., prior to May 1, 2008.

[5] Clearly, no order restraining the Canadian Forces from releasing Mr. McBride could have been made by Barnes J. once Mr. McBride had been released, as was

the case on June 12, 2007. Furthermore, insofar as this appeal is concerned, it appears that Mr. McBride was compulsorily released from the Canadian Forces at the expiry of his term of service on May 1, 2008, i.e., some four months ago.

[6] In the circumstances, this appeal is moot. Whether or not the release on June 12, 2007 was legal is an entirely different question that is not before the Court in this appeal. No valid reason was advanced by Mr. McBride which would lead the Court to hear the appeal despite its mootness.

[7] The appeal will be dismissed with costs payable to the respondent assessed at $500.

For this opportunity, we had waited almost nine months (and paid somewhere in the neighbourhood of $50,000).

Andrew had been released June 12 even if it had been illegally done—far be it for the court to rule on the legality of things, after all. And even if he hadn't been released on June 12, 2007, he had surely been released May 1, 2008, an imaginary date that came from CF and fell squarely within the time spent waiting for this half-page nugget of judicial gold.

It should be noted that compulsory release has nothing to do with term of service. Andrew had graduated from RMC on May 2, 1999. At that time he had a five-year term of service in front of him, meaning that he could not have *voluntarily* left CF prior to May 2, 2004. The Canadian Forces can and does choose to release members prior to their term of service all the time. May 1, 2008 was a date lifted from Décary's cursory understanding of materials presented by CF. When General Hillier had granted redress on the PRB release, he had suggested that Andrew be made a troop commander for two and one third years in order to prove himself. Andrew was, of course, never afforded that opportunity (because there had never been any intention that he would be afforded it) but the date May 1, 2008 would have been the end of that trial period.

Perhaps the only hint that the justices had paid sufficient attention to recognize that something smelled here came at the very end of the ruling. In assessing cost at only $500, we were let off the hook lightly. Who really knows what they were thinking? We know how they ruled, but anything beyond that is speculation.

In terms of our fight to keep Andrew in Canadian Forces, we had lost. He was out. We could perhaps have taken it to the Supreme Court, but no one liked our chances there. CF had been too slippery with their manoeuvres, and the courts seemed perfectly willing to accept Andrew's June 2007 release as a fact. And so we would wait for our FA decision from Gen Natynczyk, but first, of course, we would have to wait for the CFGB to come up with their recommendations, and they'd had it for more than two years already.

A prothonotary is a judicial officer invested with many of the powers and functions of a Federal Court Judge. They are often employed for mediation and case management. On November 21, 2008, following the vigorous efforts of Prothonotary Kevin Aalto in three different case conferences, Robert Danay, counsel for CF, agreed that CF would provide disclosure of the medical evidence. On December 5, 2008, Major J.J. Reilly, of the Office of the Judge Advocate General for Canadian Forces, disclosed the medical evidence that had been considered by the office of the D Med Pol in assigning MELs under cover of a letter stating that:

> "The following represents a summary of the best available information regarding the basis for the decisions to impose medical limitations and to release McBride."

Enclosed with the letter were copies of the specific medical reports containing this evidence. Thirty-one pages of material. It was some three years since I had first requested disclosure. Canadian Forces did not, however, disclose the policy guidelines which had been used by D Med Pol in assigning the MELs to this medical evidence, and the guidelines were the other half of the equation.

The evidence disclosed by JAG was the specific medical evidence we had repeatedly requested. We had, in the meantime, also obtained a copy of his *complete* medical file. Now that we had both, we sat down to compare what we had received from JAG with that in the medical file. What we discovered were two distinct stories.

First, there was the one presented to Director Military Careers Administration and Resource Management prior to his AR/MEL decision to release Andrew. This story was the one CF had presented to the courts through numerous proceedings and included a February 2005 opinion of Dr. Ewing, the psychiatrist at CFB Borden assessing and treating Andrew. Even in that opinion, Dr. Ewing had made it clear that:

> "It is my opinion that the initial and ongoing symptoms are a consequence of the conflicts with the military over his career."

While the fact that he tied Andrew's condition to the grievance process was not ideal from CF's perspective, it included the phrase *ongoing symptoms* which was useful.

The second story (the more complete story) included, among other things, Dr. Ewing's *later* opinion following the Gen Hillier's grant of redress in January 2006. Ewing had observed an improvement in Andrew's condition in a Consultation Report dated February 24, 2006. This suppressed report would have been more problematic:

> "With the turn of events, it is possible that he may become employable and deployable once again."

...which is precisely why it never saw LCol Taillefer's desk.

It was now *very* clear why they fought disclosure so fiercely. They had carefully cherry-picked evidence. Indeed there was plenty to suggest that a MELs decision should have, according to CF policy, been sent back to D Med Pol for reassessment. CF chose not to do this precisely because their use of the MELs process was never genuine from the start but merely a means to an end.

—

Needless to say, it is impossible to see into the future. As individuals with distant targets, we take aim and launch ourselves forward, trusting in our own abilities to carry us towards our intended goals. But our trajectories are ever subject to outside forces beyond our control.

In the summer of 2001, Andrew McBride and Michelle Knight were both second lieutenants with promising careers ahead of them. Captain Dan Bobbitt was Andrew's course officer at CTC Gagetown. Michelle Knight was the subject of a heated exchange between Dan Bobbitt and Andrew McBride which may or may not have contributed to a simmering enmity between them.

In 2009, Andrew McBride, never having been afforded a chance at the career he had grown up hoping to pursue, was on the outside looking in. Major Dan Bobbitt was promoted to Lieutenant Colonel. And Maj Michelle Mendes (née Knight), for reasons that remain unclear to this day, took her own life in an airbase outside of Kandahar.

Fourteen

On December 6, 2010, eighteen months after becoming CDS, General Walter Natynczyk rendered his FA response on the MELs and MELs release, the CFGB recommendations—more than three and a half years in the making—having been on his desk since April.

Gen Natynczyk was aware that Dr. Ewing held the opinion that there was doubt as to whether the imposition of permanent MELs continued to be correct and also that a second opinion was required.

The CDS did not, however, refer the evidence back to D Med Pol for reassessment, in accordance with CF policy and despite CF's commitments to Andrew that it would do so. In his December 6 response, General Natynczyk exercised his *own* best medical judgment as to Andrew's prognosis and concluded Andrew had not provided the medical evidence sufficient to have convinced CF authorities (D Med Pol) that his MELs were not a true reflection of his medical condition.

It hardly needs to be pointed out that the CDS is not a physician; the D Med Pol, however, is a physician and is the designate within CF to assign MELs and to undertake any reconsideration of them. The CDS could not claim the evidence Andrew produced would not have convinced CF authorities since he had chosen not to ask them.

It was curious as well that disclosures from the CFGB and the CDS showed that someone at CF had edited the record forwarded to the CDS by deleting, in three places, my representations dated March 25, 2009, wherein I referenced the *Lamer Report* and the Former Chief Justice's opinion on the grievance process. Apparently someone concluded that *that* should not be put before the CDS, notwithstanding the CFGB's referencing them in its Findings and Recommendations.

At one point in his decision the CDS stated: "Nowhere in your [March 16, 2006] representations did you mention that you were not able to gain access to your medical documents or were missing key documents." This even though the record before the CDS *did* contain my letters dated January 3, 2006 and March 13, 2006, as well as Andrew's grievances dated January 2, 2006 and January 26, 2007, all of which *screamed for disclosure.*

Not just a farce, but a farce four years in the making. Four years to basically deflect and deny that anything about the tactics of the MELs process invoked against Andrew was at all suspect. *Nothing fishy here, folks. Nope. Nothing to see. Just move along.*

All told, this tired CF dog and pony show had been playing out for more than a decade. Natynczyk's FA decision meant that the curtain had finally dropped. The only avenue left to us at this point would be judicial review.

Oddly enough, less than a year after delivering the FA decision on Andrew's MELs grievance, for an introduction to a CF report entitled *Caring For Our Own*, Gen Natynczyk would write:

> *It has been said that the manner in which a society or insti-*
> *tution treat their most vulnerable members is a hallmark*
> *of their quality. In the military, none are more vulnerable*
> *than those who are injured or become ill. For them, the*
> *duty and responsibility to care for our own resides espe-*
> *cially with the leadership of the CF, DND, and VAC. I*

assume my share of that duty and responsibility willingly and completely.

A touching sentiment, don't you think?

Fifteen

During the course of my review of the operation of Bill C-25, it became increasingly clear to me that the Canadian Forces grievance process is not working properly. [...] While the introduction of the Grievance Board has increased the perception of an impartial grievance process, the lengthy period between the initiation of a grievance and a decision by the final authority, the CDS, gives cause for serious concern. [...]

Soldiers are not second-class citizens. They are entitled to be treated with respect, and in the case of the grievance process, in a procedurally fair manner. This is a fundamental principle that must not be lost in a bureaucratic process, even a military one. Grievances involve matters such as benefits, personnel evaluation reports, postings, release from the Canadian Forces, medical issues and harassment – all matters affecting the rights, privileges and other interests of CF members. From the grievor's point of view, pursuing a grievance takes time, often costs money, and in many cases is very stressful. Further, unlike in other organizations, grievors do not have unions or employee associations through which to pursue their grievances, nor do grievors generally have recourse to the Federal Court or to the Ombudsman while a redress of grievance is within

the grievance process. It is essential to the morale of CF
members that their grievances be addressed in a fair, trans-
parent, and prompt manner.

Right Honourable Antonio Lamer P.C., C.C., C.D.
Sept 3, 2003

I had first read the Lamer report back in 2003 and had taken
heart from it. Seven years later, I hoped that the sentiment expressed
therein would resonate with a likeminded judge.

In a Judicial Review, a court limits itself to ensuring that the
procedure behind the decision has been fair: if so, it dismisses
the case; if not, it overturns the decision and sends it back for a
reconsideration to be this time in accordance with procedural fairness—that is, it will not substitute its decision for that of the original decision-maker.

We did not need to take the PRB decision to the courts because
the CF, in granting redress, had remedied that situation. With the
MELs decision, if the court found Andrew had not been afforded
procedural fairness, we argued too much time had passed and, of
course, he was long out by then, so we asked for relief in the way of
compensation for his lost wages, career, etc.

To handle the judicial review process, I went with Fritz Gaerdes
from Alexander Holburn Beaudin & Lang. Fritz is a product of
South Africa's legal training and was the second lawyer from that
country with whom I have worked during my career. I have the
utmost respect for that training as both have been fine counsel
indeed. CF went with Patrick Walker from the Department
of Justice.

There were three main points we decided to pursue in judicial review:

The first point was that CF's refusal from the very beginning
to disclose the medical evidence against Andrew and the policies

against which that evidence was weighed meant that we were never able to mount a proper defence. The importance of disclosure is so obvious that no good explanation other than the deliberate handicapping of our defence could be made. Certainly, CF had never bothered to offer a credible alternate explanation for their refusal.

Second: The Chief of the Defence Staff, General Natynczyk, was not qualified to render medical judgements of the evidence before him in the grievance and should have gone back to the Director of Medical Policy for his opinion. But the Director of Medical Policy had, in more than five years, never once been given updated medical information on Andrew's case, contrary to policies that suggested he ought to have been. This was highly conspicuous and, to my mind, called into question the true motives of the original assessment, the timing of which was suspect to begin with.

Finally, the repeated and protracted delays, especially when set against the seemingly inexorable forward momentum of the release process, not to mention the timing and tactics of the so-called June 2007 release, were inexcusable. It took almost five years to navigate the grievance process and not all of that can be conveniently laid at the feet of the CFGB.

The application to the Federal Court was filed on January 11, 2011.

We made one last attempt at disclosure, this time trying to force CF's hands to disclose the numerous orders and policies which would have been reviewed, considered and/or relied upon by the CF physicians in making the decision to impose MELs. Gaerdes made one last request for disclosure in a letter to Walker dated February 24, 2011; it was refused.

As it turns out, we managed to get our hands on a copy of the guidelines through other means. There had been a recent decision which set what we thought was a fairly clear precedent in terms of our second point.

Smith v. Canada (National Defence) 2010 FC 321 ruled that the CDS was not qualified to render medical opinions. In July of 2006, CDS General Rick Hillier had declined to follow the recommendations of the CFGB in the case of Lt(N) Catherine Ann Smith and ruled on evidence that ought to have been sent to the D Med Pol for reassessment. The D Med Pol was also called onto the carpet for not following its own guidelines set out in a document known as *Pearls of Wisdom.*

When Gaerdes saw that, he requested the file be brought in to the Registry from Ontario so he could look through it to see whether it contained a copy of *Pearls of Wisdom.* It did, and that's ultimately how we got our hands on it.

Reading through *Pearls of Wisdom,* it became pretty clear why CF had refused to disclose it. The guidelines set out in *Pearls of Wisdom* made it very clear that MELs diagnoses, even so-called permanent MELs, were subject to review and stressed the need for the D Med Pol to assess new information as it came available for reassessment.

It is only reasonable to assume that *Pearls of Wisdom* causing problems for CF in Smith v. Canada (and perhaps other cases) factored into CF's refusal to disclose it to us.

The case was heard on August 2, 2011 by Justice Luc Martineau and a decision rendered on August 25, 2011. Martineau held that withholding the medical evidence and guidelines used in the imposition of MELs in question did not constitute a breach of procedural fairness. Furthermore, because the medical evidence itself had *eventually* been released to us, any breach of procedural fairness stemming from its being withheld had been addressed. It upheld the decision of the CDS, and the application was dismissed with costs.

We appealed to the Federal Court of Appeal. The appeal was filed on September 22, 2011, and heard on May 15, 2012, by Justices of Appeal Denis Pelletier, Karen Sharlow, and Robert Mainville. A decision was rendered on June 15, 2012. The Court of Appeal was far more critical of the CF, calling into question a number of their more tenuous assertions and casting their behaviour in a skeptical light. When it came to their withholding of *Pearls of Wisdom*, a document that was *according to CF* publicly available to anyone (*who knew it existed* and *where to look for it*), the Court of Appeal found it questionable and ultimately wrong-headed. But that is as far as they were willing to go. The Court of Appeal stopped short of finding any breach of procedural fairness, upheld the decision of the CDS, and the appeal was dismissed with costs.

Finally, we sought to appeal to the Supreme Court of Canada. At this level it is a two-step process: first, Gaerdes sought leave (permission) of the Court to file an appeal, and second, if leave were to have been granted, he would have then had to file the appeal itself. The application for leave was filed on September 11, 2012, and a decision rendered on December 13, 2012, by Justices Michael Moldaver, Marshall Rothstein, and Morris Fish. The application was dismissed with costs.

Since judicial review was our last resort and the Supreme Court of Canada is the highest court in the country, we had reached the end of the road. No one in the Canadian Forces would be held to account. They had won.

December 2012 also saw the retirement of General Walter John Natynczyk as CDS. He was replaced by General Thomas J. Lawson, and the treads of the CF military machine simply kept rolling ever-forward.

Part 4:
The Dust Clears

Sixteen

It is hard to accept defeat, especially when you disagree with the rulings that have handed it to you. I had fought on Andrew's behalf for more than twelve years only to fail. It had been a David and Goliath battle from the start, and in the end Goliath had been shielded from on high.

Surveying the aftermath on the battlefield was not pretty, choked as it was by the scattered ghosts of fallen weekends and lost nights beyond counting. These were twelve years I was not going to get back. Our line of credit with the bank lay in ruin, our savings decimated, and all they had purchased were thirty banker's boxes of documents that crowded my den like a cenotaph for times that might have been, vacations not taken, intimate evenings never known.

It is hard to move forward from something like that. I decided I would commit things to paper, and so I started writing. I did not know at first how to approach it, and my first attempt would bear little resemblance to the book you now hold in your hand.

—

The reason it's important to move forward, of course, is that the rest of the world never stops spinning. Life goes on. Objects in motion follow trajectories predicated by those forces that set them in motion. To stop and latch onto the past is to voluntarily allow the present and future to draw away and leave you behind.

In June of 2013, the trajectory of LCol Dan Bobbitt saw him made Commanding Officer of the 2nd Regiment, Royal Canadian Horse Artillery. This was the position held by LCol John Crosman back in 2001 when Bobbitt's accusation had derailed Andrew's career. On the one hand, it is hard to know what to make of that. On the other hand, perhaps there is nothing to be made from it at all. Trajectory. Physics is physics.

Was Dan Bobbitt to blame for what happened to Andrew?

Dan Bobbitt was a young captain in July 2001, perhaps with a chip on his shoulder (perhaps not), perhaps with a grudge against Andrew (perhaps not) and well within his rights to bring the charge that he decided (for whatever reason) to bring. Perhaps, as Col Ward later suggested, he was merely an inexperienced officer lost in the fog of war. He was overzealous in his pursuit of things and over-stepped some lines in the collection and presentation of evidence, but beyond that very little is certain.

Ultimately the blame for the initial PRB has to fall to LCol Haeck who allowed a half-baked hearing to play out in front of his eyes with little or no critical oversight. Andrew never once took issue with being forced to attend a PRB hearing. He took issue with Capt Bobbitt's characterization of events, of course, and questioned the course officer's motives in light of their fractious relationship, but this was not what the initial grievance was about. The grievance was always about how the senior officer in charge failed to exercise so much as a glimmer of discretion to ensure that the hearing was procedurally fair. LCol Haeck was responsible for the hearing and failed utterly in that duty. As if that wasn't bad enough, he then over-stepped what authority he had by reviewing his own ruling rather than passing it immediately to Col Ward.

Early on (perhaps as early as Col Ward, perhaps not) the deci-sion was likely made that the potential bad blood and mishandling meant that they didn't want Andrew around, and the decisions were less and less about the facts of the case and more and more about holding the line and dealing with what they increasingly saw as a problem/challenge. Even as early as Col Ward, granting redress to Andrew would have been a slap to LCol Haeck, his new Chief of Staff.

Ultimately, there are far too many intelligent individuals in CF for so much nonsense to have gone unrecognized. I am of the opinion that most of the apparent idiocy was not borne of stupidity but willfulness and, as Justice Pelletier would eventually put it, wrong-headedness.

Part of the problem, perhaps, is that officers pass in and out of positions so quickly that (a) they don't have time to fully assess the responsibilities and challenges and (b) their attention is never entirely on the job at hand. Part of the problem is that in a sufficiently large fluid organization, where individuals are forever inheriting the decision of their predecessors, the idea of accountability becomes fuzzy at best.

What CF seemed determined to do from day one was move ahead with its wishes while simultaneously delaying the grievance process—which is why they objected so vigorously whenever an application for a Federal Court stay was filed. A grievance process that can simply be ignored is not a grievance process at all; it is little more than theatre for the aggrieved.

The grievance process that failed Andrew was profoundly broken because it was not taken seriously by any of the officers involved. The reason it wasn't taken seriously is simple: nothing compelled them to take it seriously. My experience suggests that CF officers drawn into a grievance look at process as a nuisance, an obstacle thrown in their path, slowing them up from simply carrying out their wishes unchallenged. Unfortunately, what they perceive as obstacles and nuisances are intended to be checks and balances.

There is a disconnect here between intention and execution, between theory and practice, if you will. The grievance process is not looked upon as a process at all by the ranking officers who administer it. To them it is a procedure, and there is a difference. A procedure is a series of steps followed in order to reach a desired outcome. A process is a series of steps followed in order to determine the *proper* outcome. The military mindset is one that is built around overcoming resistance and reaching objectives, but a grievance is meant to be addressed, not merely overcome.

The revolutionary idea that Andrew's case should, at any point, be looked at with fresh eyes to see if his grievances had merit was, as I've suggested, never taken seriously. So how might you compel officers to take the process seriously? How is this for a simple first step:

Make an Administrative Review (AR) based on a PRB impossible while the grievance process on said PRB is outstanding. Furthermore, make release proceeding flowing from an AR impossible while the grievance process on said AR is outstanding. That simple common-sense policy would better compel CF to handle the process in a timely and procedurally fair manner.

A second less obvious—but perhaps even more effective—suggestion would be to have officers who carelessly (or intentionally) screw up or circumvent the grievance process officially censured by those superiors who are subsequently drawn into the process to clean up their mess in such a way that their future advancement might be impacted.

The Lamer report too made a number of very good recommendations. In his estimation, the system was *theoretically* sound but fell woefully short when that theory was put into practice. In Justice Lamer's view, the entire process, from initial grievance to final authority (were a grievance to go that far) should take no more than twelve months (and recommended that after twelve months grievors be allowed to go to the courts). You might look at many of Justice Lamer's recommendations as a tightening up of the process.

Lamer recognized in 2003 that the CFGB was a huge bottleneck and made recommendations to proactively clear out the backlog that existed. Of course, that backlog still existed in August 2006 almost three years later as was evidenced by the fact that our MELs grievance would be more than three and a half years with the CFGB before landing on Gen Natynczyk's desk (Hiller had been CDS when the CFGB first got the grievance). Lamer further recognized the need to allow the Chief of the Defence staff to delegate his role as final authority in some cases in order to allow for a timely response—Gen Natynczyk got the CFGB recommendations in April 2010 and only bothered to rule in December.

Among his other recommendations, one in particular really hit home and spoke to an issue (perhaps even *the* issue) that impacted everything that followed in Andrew's case:

> I recommend that initial authorities be given the requisite training, authority and resources in order to be able to resolve grievances.

Imagine if LCol Haeck and/or Col Ward had known how to properly assess and handle a grievance and it had stopped with them. Haeck would have known to send it to Ward initially, and Ward would have known enough to assess the issues of the grievance itself and look at the fundamental failings in the PRB for what they were rather than simply trying to stall, spin, or pass the buck. It might have gone no further than Col Ward and been put to bed as early as Christmas 2001. As it was, Andrew's struggles dragged on for another eleven years. Such a colossal waste of time and energy on everyone's part. It cost CF a good officer. It cost me and Kerry much of our life savings as well as countless hours we will never see again. And it cost Canadian taxpayers, I am sorry to say, hundreds of thousands of dollars. And all because CF refused to forego the ends they were determined to pursue for so much as a moment in order to give their means a sober second look. Pure madness.

—

By Christmas 2013, I had finished the first draft of a manuscript, but I was unsure what to make of it. It lacked a cohesive structure, and I didn't know how it would be received. It was quite technical in places, and though forcefully argued, in retrospect I realize that it often read as though it was being directed towards the courts. The problem was that the courts had already ruled. Just who was I writing for? Who was my audience? That first manuscript looped back on itself a number of times and spent a great deal of energy spinning its wheels.

Early on I had bounced the idea of my writing this book off a neighbour of ours. A wise bookseller with years of experience, her big question was whether the book would be readable. It was a good question. What I had done was attempt to distill those thirty boxes of documents into something that could be bottled in a manuscript. Had I succeeded? Was it readable?

I knew Kerry wanted me to find a way to put the past twelve years to bed so I could step away from it and move on. I couldn't blame her. This book was how I was going to do that, but I wasn't sure I had accomplished what I set out to do, and I was too close to it to see things clearly.

I needed an outside reader.

I was fortunate to find an excellent editor in Victoria who agreed to evaluate the manuscript and give me some objective feedback. He confirmed my worst fears. What I had written was not really readable. It was lucid enough, of course, but it lacked context and was not compelling. And while this was disheartening, I knew it was true. What he said next, however, would be a game changer.

"Y'know, this really is a terrific story, and I can see that even just catching occasional glimpses of it. People connect to stories naturally, far more naturally than they connect to issues. Personally I think your best bet would be to simply approach it like a memoir, a story. Laying it out as a story also has the benefit of providing you with a rock solid infrastructure insofar as a story unfolds in chronological order. You can still touch on all the issues you want to talk about, but you simply resign yourself to talking about them as they relate to the story as it plays out."

That was a lightbulb moment, and as soon as I sat back down to approach a new manuscript, I could see what he meant. The story itself was nowhere in the thirty bankers boxes even though the contents of those boxes had been generated by the story. I had a number of conversations with my editor over the months and he was a huge help as the manuscript progressed. In fact, he would be the one who came up with the idea of trajectory as a theme.

—

The Wainwright Garrison is located 210 kilometres east of Edmonton and is home to two major training centres. On May 21, 2014, there was an accident during Ex MAPLE RESOLVE, one of the largest training exercises of the year. A Light Armoured Vehicle (LAV III) crossing some rough terrain overturned. Four soldiers in the LAV III were injured, and their commanding officer, LCol Dan Bobbitt was killed.

It was not the first such rollover with the LAV III. Indeed, Private Patrick Dessureault was killed in a similar accident at Wainwright in 2005. CF will not go so far as to question the safety of Canada's LAV III but admit that, at over seventeen thousand kilograms, it has a relatively high centre of gravity. Shortly after the incident, military analyst Col Michel Drapeau (Ret'd) suggested that the cause of the deadly rollover was likely attributable to human error or lack of experience with the vehicle.

LCol Bobbitt's military career spanned twenty-three years. He died as the Commanding Officer of the 2nd Regiment, Royal Canadian Horse Artillery.

Epilogue

In November, Peter Ramsay and I headed up to Cortes Island for our annual work party to clear the power line of trees. We'd purchased the property back in 1974 before Peter and I left Strongitharm Miller Currie & Ramsay—a hundred and twenty acres of forested waterfront on the eastern shore of Cortes, looking out on Desolation Sound, just south of Squirrel Cove—and trips like this date back forty years.

We left Nanaimo early and hit Campbell River just before seven. We rented an industrial chipper, hitched it to Peter's truck and easily made the 7:30 ferry to Qauthiaski Cove on Quadra. Though my instinct was to drive straight to Heriot Bay to make the lineup for the 9:05 ferry to Whaletown, I let Peter talk me into coffee and some breakfast first. Peter has in recent years become a slave to his coffee.

As it turns out we were almost out of luck when we reached Heriot Bay. There was a long lineup, and it did not look promising. Peter was starting to sweat, knowing full well that I would never let him live it down if we had to wait around for the 11:05 ferry. In fact, the only reason we ended up making the sailing at all is that the ferry captain did not like the look of the three cement trucks that had come into Qauthiaski Cove with us—and had *not* stopped for coffee—deeming the load too heavy for an otherwise full sailing that already included a logging truck and so pulled us out of the line. Ours was the last vehicle allowed on.

Though Peter and I had a lot of work ahead of us, I was looking forward to it as I always do. Two doughty lawyers in their late sixties returning to the wild—even if it is a quasi-civilized wild—to put things in order. It's always good to get away.

Earlier in the week, when I had told Peter I was bringing the manuscript with me, he joked that he wouldn't get a lick of work out of me.

"My God, have you not finished that thing yet?"

"It's done," I said, though not entirely sure myself. "Or at least I think it is. But I want to review it, and it needs an epilogue of some sort before I send it out for copyediting."

"I can't imagine what you'll do with yourself once you put it to bed."

"I know what you mean," I said.

The drive across Cortes to the property is always somewhat magical for me. Though it has changed in forty years, that change is nowhere near as pronounced as in Nanaimo. And there is a real sense of connection to an earlier time in my life, one when I was a young lawyer, newly married and just embarking on a career. Even today, looking out on Desolation Sound, I cannot help but catch glimpses of Andrew and Stephan as small kids happily manning their Navy Base and dreaming of what life held in store for them.

When we arrived at the property we unloaded our stuff and then got right to work.

We would sleep in the main cabin, but my plan was to rise early each morning to review the manuscript and try to gather up the last of my thoughts. The first night, before turning in, I set up my papers and a coffeemaker in the adjoining guest cottage. I woke at four, which is no great hardship for me as I am naturally an early riser, got dressed and stepped outside. It was still fully dark, of course, and chilly, but it felt good to open up the cottage, pour myself a cup of coffee and set to work. Dawn was still three hours away.

I started reading and scrawling occasional notes in the margins of the printed pages and was struck by the imminent sense of closure at the prospect of stepping away from all for good. There was a sense of exhilaration that I suspect would be familiar to marathon runners, but at the same time an overwhelming exhaustion at the thought of it all.

At first I had stepped forward to help Andrew navigate what I thought would be a fairly straightforward grievance process. I look back now and that seems naïve, but I took CF at their word. By the end, I was simply fighting for some sort of settlement from the courts to recognize that what had been done was not in line with Canadian values.

In some ways I am more disappointed with the court system that ultimately let CF walk away from their responsibilities. This is a story which speaks for itself, and a second-year law student with one eye closed could see that Andrew had not been afforded procedural fairness, and yet CF was allowed to skate off without penalty.

I think that's what really stings.

Andrew's case was not complicated, despite CF's attempts to paint it as such. What we were arguing was very clear, but at every step we were met with stonewalling, deception, mischaracterization and diversion. I refuse to believe that courts could not see what was going on—to do so would be to assume a bench warmed by simpletons. I have to assume that I happened to draw judges who were simply reluctant to stand up and call a spade a spade. An individual going up against an opponent as powerful as the Canadian Forces is at a fundamental disadvantage, and everyone in the courtroom recognizes that. And yet the courts, at just about every turn, decided to make soft calls in CF's favour.

I learned a lot about the Canadian Forces and how they operate both internally and within a court of law. The Canadian Forces, however, learned nothing whatsoever. There was an opportunity perhaps for a lesson on Canadian values and procedural fairness, but the courts shirked that responsibility and decided not to present them with it. Instead the powers that be within the Canadian Forces were allowed to reaffirm that might is right and that ends justify the means.

Andrew's aspirations of a military career didn't simply rain down from the sky when he was a child. Ours was a family with long-standing ties to the military both in Canada and abroad. Andrew's dreams grew from a rich soil of family tradition. And when Andrew expressed a desire to join the Canadian Forces he found broad support from his family. That same support would not be forth-coming today. I would have a hard time comfortably endorsing the Canadian Forces as a wise choice for a young person coming to me for advice. What could I possibly say?

> "It's a rewarding lifestyle that will challenge you to achieve… unless of course you accidentally cross the wrong person and the rest of them turn on you."

> "It's a chance to make a meaningful contribution… if you're lucky enough to navigate your way through a career where you are never at odds with any decision affecting you."

> "It's a chance to serve your country… in a rigid top-down institution that, if push comes to shove, won't afford you the rights afforded other Canadians."

Canada's military has a role to play on the world stage and will for the foreseeable future. For that reason recruitment is important, and as the population becomes more connected and stories and experiences become readily available through things like self-pub-lishing and social media, the Canadian Forces is going to have to start living up to their mandates in terms of how they treat the men and women serving in its ranks.

The military (and this is true of all militaries) is large and con-servative and run by men (for the most part) who have lived and breathed its traditions for years and years. While it can be argued that traditions make an organization strong, the flip side is that it makes an organization resistant to change because those in a position to implement change have often benefited from some of the traditions that need changing. That's not to say that those in power are responsible for the system through which they rose, but it does mean that they need to look outside of the traditions and mindsets that have served them and ask if something else might better serve those coming up behind them.

What am I trying to achieve by writing all this?

Hopefully this is more than simply a coda to the last thirteen years of my life. It is, of course, my attempt to put things to bed and move on with my life as I've said, but hopefully it is more than that. More than anything I want to add my voice to voices like those of Justice Lamer who recognize the need for fundamental change within the Canadian Forces. It is my hope that by presenting this story as I have, in its entirety and with as much context as possible, I am contributing to a conversation that needs to happen.

This is what happened to Andrew. This is how he was treated. This is what the Canadian Forces was allowed to do. This is a single snapshot of our military—and though it's not flattering, it's true nonetheless.

Are there good people in the Canadian Forces? Of course there are.

Are the men and women of the Canadian Forces working to promote and protect Canadian values around the world? Yes they are, and they should be held in high esteem for doing so.

All that being said, are the Canadian Forces as rigorous when it comes to promotion and protection of Canadian values when it comes to how it treats its own members? There are numerous stories, not just Andrew's, to suggest that they're not.

And there are no good reasons why they shouldn't.

—

At a quarter after seven it starts to get light outside and I get up to stretch.

I walk over to the window and, looking out over the water, I am reminded of the scope of life. When confined to a map, Desolation Sound is a small blue shape, but the reality of it is vast, full of possibility and wonder. A memoir is very much the same way. It is life scaled down to the size of a book. So much is left out.

Andrew was twenty-four when Capt Dan Bobbitt accused him of lying. As I write this in November 2014, he is thirty-seven, and to pretend that I have captured the last thirteen-plus years of his life in a forty-thousand word manuscript would be ridiculous.

Andrew is engaged to a woman he met at RMC in the spring of 2007. He and Nancy lived together for a while in a rented house in Kingston and, in 2008, pulled up stakes and moved to Japan for a while where Andrew further pursued his Aikido.

It is funny how things worked out with Aikido. Andrew first picked it up at RMC while pursuing a military career, and when he injured his foot in 1998 and had to miss his BAO III, he spent a great deal of that summer instead working on Aikido. The Canadian Forces turned on Andrew, and he was eventually forced out, but Andrew's enthusiasm for Aikido never faltered, and he now teaches and travels with some of the top Aikido practitioners in the world. In fact, though he and Nancy moved back to Burnaby a couple of years ago, as I write this Andrew is back in Japan for an Aikido seminar. Last month it was Brazil, next fall it will be Europe. Whatever Andrew does, he throws himself into it.

He'd have made a hell of an officer. Though he gave it his best shot, he simply landed elsewhere.

Appendix

FULL STEAM AHEAD!

The *McBride* decision and the boondoggle of the CF
Career Administrative Review process ten years on

by Michel W. Drapeau & Joshua M. Juneau
Esprit de Corps Vol. 21, Issue 5 (June 2014)

In our practice, we have seen, time and time again, soldiers who have been recommended for release through an improper administrative review process. Prior to actual release, we assist the soldier to file a grievance concerning procedural safeguards that were abused or ignored, and lack of due process afforded by the Canadian Armed Forces administration in the release procedure. Our experience has been that, initially, these grievances are largely ignored by the CAF bureaucracy who continues to move, at full throttle, to release that soldier, despite legitimate concerns raised through their grievance.

In cases where the grievance is upheld after that soldier has been released, the Canadian Armed Forces administration is left with a procedural nightmare: they are required to place the soldier in a position that they would have been in had the injustices never occurred — a tort remedy. This often requires having to undo and untangle years of administrative boondoggling, annuity adjustments, salary and promotion adjustments, benefit adjustments — plus interest of course — and restoration of that person's reputation. This is no easy feat. Realistically, the person's reputation can never fully be rehabilitated; their professional reputation and sense of trust and confidence in the chain of command likely would have been eroded and suffered irreparable harm.

As early as 2004, the federal court recognized that the Canadian Armed Forces administrative review process is imperfect, and often conducted in a hasty, biased and unfair manner. It appears that, despite the passage of over ten years since the federal court raised this concern, the Canadian Armed Forces is unwilling to address this issue and make changes to their policies and procedures. The following case study of the 2004 federal court decision in *McBride* may help to illustrate the point.

Some Things Never Change

In 2001 Second Lieutenant (2Lt) Robert Andrew McBride was at the Combat Training Center at Canadian Armed Forces Base Gagetown, training to become an artillery officer. As field exercises were wrapping up, 2Lt McBride was assigned to the position of Gun Position Officer. Among his duties were to ensure that the battery personnel were awake and ready to commence training at the appropriate time in the mornings.

On the evening prior to the final day of training, after having checked with his superior, 2Lt McBride set the reveille for the troops for 0600 hrs, and went to bed.

To his surprise, the following morning at 0530 hrs, 2Lt McBride was awoken by his Course Officer who stated that the timings had changed and that the next phase of operations was due to *commence* at 0600 hrs. Allegedly, this situation report was communicated to 2Lt McBride the night before; however, 2Lt McBride did not remember ever receiving such a report, and told the course instructor same.

It should be noted that the effect of improperly setting the reveille ended up being an operational or training *non sequitor*, as 2Lt McBride 'rallied the troops' and ensured that his battery made their timings to their position at 0600 hrs.

Remarkably, at the conclusion of the day's training, 2Lt McBride was the subject of an incident report for lying to his Course Officer, an overeager Captain Bobbitt, for stating that he did not remember receiving a situation report the night before.

PRB Convened

As a consequence of Capt Bobbitt's incident report, a progress review board was convened, chaired by the Commandant of the artillery school, Lieutenant Colonel (LCol) Haeck, to consider whether or not 2Lt McBride was suitable for further employment as an officer in the Canadian Armed Forces.

Despite limited evidence against him, LCol Haeck found 2Lt McBride guilty of lying, failed him on the course, made him cease training immediately, and recommended 2Lt McBride for immediate release from the Canadian Armed Forces — all on the balance of probabilities.

Grievance

In October 2001, 2Lt McBride filed a grievance that the recommendations of the PRB were heavy handed and inappropriate in the circumstances. This grievance specifically concerned the actions of the commandant, LCol Haeck, as chairman of the noted PRB, and as remedy, 2Lt McBride requested that the recommendation for release be overturned and that he be permitted to continue training as an officer in the Canadian Armed Forces.

Despite that this grievance was addressed to his commanding officer, 2 RCHA, remarkably, it was sent to the LCol Haeck, who decided to determine this grievance personally; this despite the obvious conflict of interest, lack of impartiality, and procedural prohibition of individuals handling appeals of his own prior decisions.

Somewhat predictably, the commandant refused to overturn his own original decision and denied 2Lt McBride's grievance. This should come as no surprise.

Full Steam Ahead!

By June 2002, 2Lt McBride was *"de facto* released" in that he was removed from the guns and placed in a supervised position. Furthermore, an officer slate was prepared showing "release" adjacent to his name. In response to his treatment, in November 2002, 2Lt McBride filed another grievance concerning the actions of his chain of command in intentionally limiting his career progression without merit.

This grievance was sent to the (then) Canadian Armed Forces Grievance Board, now the Military Grievances External Review Committee, for findings and recommendations.

Administrative Review

While his grievance was being reviewed, in February 2003, 2Lt McBride was subjected to a career administrative review to determine whether or not he was suitable to continue serving with the Canadian Armed Forces. The reason for having the administrative review cited that 2Lt McBride allegedly lied to his course officer way back in 2001!

2Lt McBride prepared an objection. There was no hearing, and in June 2003 2Lt McBride was recommended for release from the Canadian Armed Forces.

Grievance Of Improper Release

In November 2002, 2Lt McBride filed a grievance concerning the decision to release him, citing procedural deficiencies, lack of due process, false accusations, and irreparable harm. Despite this 2Lt McBride was advised that the administrative review would proceed — full steam ahead!

In reply, after having spoken to a civilian lawyer, 2Lt McBride filed a judicial review to the federal court seeking an order restraining the Canadian Armed Forces from releasing him prior to rendering a decision on his grievance.

McBride V. CDS

2Lt McBride applied to the federal court to have his release stayed pending determination of his grievance. To prove his case, 2Lt McBride applied the test from *Manitoba v. Metropolitan Stores* [1987] 1 SCR 110, showing the relative strength of his case, irreparable harm and demonstrating the balance of convenience favoured his retention until the grievance was decided. Specifically, 2Lt McBride argued that the Canadian Armed Forces:

- Failed in their duty to act fairly, despite knowledge of this duty;

- Intentionally ignored and delayed its own procedures;

- Made false accusations against 2Lt McBride;

- Did not give 2Lt McBride the right to notice, disclosure, protection of oral hearing, right to present evidence, right to legal counsel, right to impartial decision maker, the right to have redress not be redundant etc;

- Would cause 2Lt McBride irreparable harm if permitted to proceed with his release;

- Wrongly broadened the charges;

- Made several errors and omissions;

- Sought to build evidence improperly (piling on) against 2Lt McBride;

- Made several unprofessional and unbecoming personal attacks on 2Lt McBride;

- Used tactics of haste and delay;

- Ignored 2Lt McBride's request to hold release

The court sided with 2Lt McBride preventing the Canadian Armed Forces from releasing him until the grievance had been determined, with costs of course.

Why Is This Happening?

The fault in the administrative review process may lay with the broken Canadian Armed Forces grievance process. Consider that, currently, the average time for a grievance to be determined at the initial authority level is more than 180 days — this is the *average,* and despite that the *Queens Regulations and Orders* attach a 60-day time limit to decide grievances at the initial authority.

Under the *National Defence Act,* there is no statutory provision compelling the chief of the defence staff or his delegate acting as the final authority to ever decide a grievance. Not surprisingly, this has caused an unacceptable back log in grievance determinations, and at least one grievance that we're aware of has been sitting on the chief of the defence staff's desk for nearly four years.

If grievances were handled in a timely manner, as proscribed by statute, they would be determined inside the time on a release message. As the current grievance system operates, if this were to happen today, 2Lt McBride could see an indeterminate retention in the Canadian Armed Forces, while his grievance grinds its way through the system — a system which takes years to resolve even the most basic of complaints.

More *à propos* the chief of the defence staff is supposed to be the final authority in all Canadian Armed Forces grievances. The purpose for this is that the chief of the defence staff maintains awareness of morale and concerns of the lower ranks, instead of being insulated by senior members who notoriously produce rose coloured reports. More recently, the chief of the defence staff is failing in this task, by delegating his role as the final authority to other senior members, usually holding the rank of colonel.

Conclusion

Time and time again, we have heard the military repeat the adage "people are our most important asset." Notwithstanding the indignity of referring to people as chattels, in terms of the administrative review procedure, the Canadian Armed Forces is not walking the talk.

If their people are so important, the Canadian Armed Forces would have learned a valuable lesson in 2004 when the federal court decided *McBride.* In response to this landmark decision, the Canadian Armed Forces should have made changes to help ensure that the dignity of their membership remains their foremost priority. To our knowledge, they have not.

Time and time again, we have represented clients facing career administrative review recommending release, citing analogous concerns as argued by 2Lt McBride. The only administrative recourse available to these soldiers is to file a grievance and then possibly initiate a judicial review before the federal court.

Perhaps it is time for the federal court to revisit *McBride.* Alternately, this problem could be mitigated if the Canadian Armed Forces followed their own grievance procedure, and the initial authority rendered a decision within 60 days. However, for an institution as resistant to change as the Canadian Armed Forces, such introspection is unlikely, and we assume that the tradition of administrative boondoggling will only continue — full steam ahead!

If you have a story of administrative snafus from the Canadian Armed Forces, we would love to hear from you. Please send your testimonial to: info@mdlo.ca. We will post the best answers, anonymously, on our website at www.mdlo.ca.

http://mdlo.ca/wp-content/uploads/2014/06/21-5-Law-Oder-McBride-decision.pdf

The Mohamed Harkat Case

Canada (Citizenship and Immigration) v. Harkat, 2014 SCC 37

Mohamed Harkat was arrested in 2002 for suspected ties to terrorism. CSIS (Canadian Security Intelligence Service) claimed he immigrated to Canada in 1995 under false pretences and that he was an al-Qaeda sleeper agent. His arrest and subsequent imprisonment pending deportation were under a security certificate which meant that the evidence against him was allowed to be kept secret.

He was released, under strict conditions, in 2006 prior to a Supreme Court case on the constitutionality of security certificates. In 2008, CSIS was ordered to disclose their evidence against Mohamed Harkat to Harkat's lawyer. They had to be ordered a second time in 2009 before they eventually complied, and even then they provided only copies of the evidence claiming that the original evidence had all been destroyed.

In 2014, the Harkat case was back in front of the Supreme Court of Canada. The government claimed Mr. Harkat was a threat to national security, and the trial judge concluded he was. The issue before the Supreme Court of Canada was whether the security certificate issued under the *Immigration and Refugee Protection Act* was sufficiently fair to Mr. Harkat. The court found that it was.

Chief Justice McLachlin addressed the issue of fair process in her judgement.

Pursuant to the principles of fundamental justice, a person named must be provided with a fair process. At issue in the present appeal are two interrelated aspects of the right to a fair process: the right to know and meet the case, and the right to have a decision made by the judge on the facts and the law. The named person must "be informed of the case against him or her, and be permitted to respond to that case". Correlatively, the named person's knowledge of the case and participation in the process must be sufficient to result in the designated judge being "exposed to the whole factual picture" of the case and having the ability to apply the relevant law to those facts.

https://scc-csc.lexum.com/scc-csc/scc-csc/en/item/13643/index.do

It can hardly be clearer than that. Fundamental justice requires that accused know the facts of the case against them so that they can properly meet the case and so the judge can be given a whole factual picture of the case in front of them.

Though Harkat's appeal was denied, it is worth noting that the courts afforded him everything he needed to meet the case against him.

In Andrew's case, we had asked CF for due process and disclosure time and time again. We wanted nothing more than evidence-based decisions from day one. This is what the Supreme Court concluded was essential to fair process in the Harkat case. In applying the principles of fundamental justice in cases involving alleged terrorists, are those principles then to be denied in cases involving those who put on the uniform to fight terrorists? The Court had an opportunity to address this in Andrew's case but failed to do so.

Concise Timeline

Jul 31, 2001   Accusation by Capt Bobbitt

Aug 1, 2001   PRB hearing

Aug 8, 2001   PRB decision [LCol Haeck]
                       — PRB grievance Oct 24, 2001

Dec 21, 2001   IA PRB response [LCol Haeck]
                       — Amended PRB grievance Apr 3, 2002

Jul 31, 2002   Second IA PRB response [Col Ward]
                       — Amended PRB grievance Nov 18, 2002

Jun 23, 2003   PRB (release) decision [BGen Hussey]
                       — PRB (release) grievance Nov 28, 2003

Jun 21, 2004   IA PRB (release) decision [MGen Hussey]
                       — Federal Court application for Stay Jun 21, 2004

Jun 29, 2004   Federal Court Stay of release pending
FA PRB granted [Kelen]

Oct 20, 2005   MELs decision (D Med Pol) [Maj Garand]
— *MELs grievance Jan 2, 2006*

Jan 12, 2006   FA PRB & PRB (release) decisions
[Gen Hillier, CDS]

Apr 18, 2006   MELs (release) decision [LCol
Taillefer, DMCARM]

Dec 1, 2006   Actual receipt of MELs (release) decision
— *MELs (release) grievance Jan 26, 2007*

Jun 12, 2007   Claimed release date
— *Federal Court Application for Stay of
Release pending FA MELs Jun 19, 2007*

Dec 14, 2007   Federal Court Stay of Release pending FA
MELs dismissed [Barnes]
— *Court of Appeal (Stay of Release
pending FA MELs)Dec 24, 2007*

Sept 16, 2008   Court of Appeal (Stay of Release pending
FA MELs) dismissed [Décary]

Dec 6, 2010   FA MELs & MELs (release) decisions [Gen
Natynczyk, CDS]
— *Federal Court Application for
Judicial Review Jan 11, 2010*

Aug 25, 2011   Federal Court Application for Judicial Review
dismissed [Martineau]
— *Court of Appeal (Application for
Judicial Review) Sept 22, 2011*

June 15, 2012   Court of Appeal (Application for Judicial
Review) dismissed [Pelletier]
— *Supreme Court Application for
Leave to Appeal Sept 11, 2012*

Dec 13, 2012   Supreme Court application for
leave to appeal dismissed

Further Reading

Independent Review of Bill C-25 Right Honourable Antonio
Lamer (Sept 3, 2003)
http://mgerc-ceegm.gc.ca/documents/lamer-eng.pdf

"Soldier's death at Kandahar base cloaked in mystery" (CBC News:
May 12, 2009)
http://www.cbc.ca/news
/canada/soldier-s-death-
at-kandahar-base-cloaked-in-mystery-1.818609

"Lieutenant-Colonel Dan Bobbitt: a soldier, a
father, a friend" (CF Article: May 23, 2014)

http://www.army-armee.forces.gc.ca/en/news-publications/
national-news-details-no-menu.page?doc=lieutenant-
colonel-dan-bobbitt-a-soldier-a-father-a-friend/
hvj86uze

Acknowledgements

I look upon this book as closure to a thirteen-year ordeal that started in the summer of 2001. As much as I often felt like a lone voice in the wilderness, I cannot pretend for a moment that I don't owe a great many people thanks for their support along the way.

This was especially true once the battle shifted to the courts. It was a pleasure to observe the skill that senior counsel brought to the task: Peter Ramsay QC in the applications for a stay, Douglas Schmitt in the appeal of the Barnes dismissal, and Fritz Gaerdes in the application and appeals for judicial review.

Being a lawyer myself, I know how getting product out the door is dependent on the skill and dedication of our legal assistants. So it was in this case, Michele Monroe at Ramsay Lampman Rhodes and Jennifer Twigg at Alexander Holburn Beaudin & Lang.

I want to thank my wife Kerry for remaining supportive of me (and our son) year after year and Andrew for hanging in there through it all and having faith in a process that ultimately failed him.

It is worth pointing out that I spoke with many CF members along the way who expressed genuine regret for CF's treatment of Andrew. While they weren't in positions to change things in Andrew's case, they made it clear they would if they could. Given the lonely road being travelled, it was reassuring and appreciated.

Finally, I would like to thank Warren Layberry of DarkWater Editing in Victoria BC. His substantive and ongoing contribution to the process helped shape the final manuscript.

About the Author

Douglas McBride has practised law on Vancouver Island for more than forty years. Politically active, he has been a board member and chair of municipal, provincial and federal boards. He and his wife Kerry live in Nanaimo, British Columbia. This is his first book.

Lightning Source UK Ltd.
Milton Keynes UK
UKOW04n2048010216

267566UK00002B/17/P